# Emptiness

Guan

# Contents

**Unsurpassed complete enlightenment**      1

Suffering . . . . . . . . . . . . . . . . . . . . . . . . . . . . . 1

The end of ignorance . . . . . . . . . . . . . . . . . . . . . 1

Unsurpassed complete enlightenment . . . . . . . . . . . . 1

The resolve to attain enlightenment . . . . . . . . . . . . 2

The bodhisattva way . . . . . . . . . . . . . . . . . . . . . 2

The six perfections . . . . . . . . . . . . . . . . . . . . . . 3

The perfection of giving . . . . . . . . . . . . . . . . . . . 3

The perfection of discipline . . . . . . . . . . . . . . . . . 3

The perfection of endurance . . . . . . . . . . . . . . . . . 3

The perfection of vigor . . . . . . . . . . . . . . . . . . . . 4

The perfection of meditation . . . . . . . . . . . . . . . . 4

The perfection of wisdom . . . . . . . . . . . . . . . . . . 4

The other shore . . . . . . . . . . . . . . . . . . . . . . . . 4

The bodhisattva way . . . . . . . . . . . . . . . . . . . . . 5

**The five skandhas and eighteen sense realms**      6

The five skandhas . . . . . . . . . . . . . . . . . . . . . . . 6

The eighteen sense realms . . . . . . . . . . . . . . . . . . 6

The eighteen sense realms . . . . . . . . . . . . . . . . . . 6

**Inherent existence**      7

Entities . . . . . . . . . . . . . . . . . . . . . . . . . . . . . 7

Inherent existence . . . . . . . . . . . . . . . . . . . . . . . 7

Inherent existence . . . . . . . . . . . . . . . . . . . . . . . 7

Endowed with inherent existence . . . . . . . . . . . . . . 7

Endowed with inherent existence . . . . . . . . . . . . . . 7

Endowed with inherent existence . . . . . . . . . . . . . . 8

Perception . . . . . . . . . . . . . . . . . . . . . . . . . . . 8

Inseparable . . . . . . . . . . . . . . . . . . . . . . . . . . . 8

Inseparable . . . . . . . . . . . . . . . . . . . . . . . . . . . 8

Inseparable . . . . . . . . . . . . . . . . . . . . . . . . . . . 8

Independently existent entities . . . . . . . . . . . . . . . 9

Separate and distinct entities . . . . . . . . . . . . . . . . . . 9

Entities . . . . . . . . . . . . . . . . . . . . . . . . . . . . . 9

Entities . . . . . . . . . . . . . . . . . . . . . . . . . . . . . 9

Forests, mountains, and rivers . . . . . . . . . . . . . . . . . 10

**The emptiness of entities**       **11**

All is empty . . . . . . . . . . . . . . . . . . . . . . . . . . . 11

The emptiness of entities . . . . . . . . . . . . . . . . . . . 11

The emptiness of entities . . . . . . . . . . . . . . . . . . . 11

The emptiness of entities . . . . . . . . . . . . . . . . . . . 11

The true nature of all . . . . . . . . . . . . . . . . . . . . . 11

Devoid of inherent existence . . . . . . . . . . . . . . . . . . 12

Devoid of inherent existence . . . . . . . . . . . . . . . . . . 12

Devoid of inherent existence . . . . . . . . . . . . . . . . . . 12

Perception . . . . . . . . . . . . . . . . . . . . . . . . . . . . 12

**The emptiness of compositions**       **13**

The emptiness of compositions . . . . . . . . . . . . . . . . 13

Forests, mountains, and rivers . . . . . . . . . . . . . . . . . 14

Contemplation . . . . . . . . . . . . . . . . . . . . . . . . . 15

**The fundamental absence of entities**       **16**

The fundamental absence of entities . . . . . . . . . . . . . 16

The true nature of all . . . . . . . . . . . . . . . . . . . . . 16

The fundamental absence of entities . . . . . . . . . . . . . 16

The fundamental absence of entities . . . . . . . . . . . . . 16

Water in a vessel . . . . . . . . . . . . . . . . . . . . . . . . 17

Entities are not entities . . . . . . . . . . . . . . . . . . . . 17

**The fundamental absence of compositions**       **18**

The fundamental absence of compositions . . . . . . . . . . . 18

Forests, mountains, and rivers . . . . . . . . . . . . . . . . . 18

Contemplation . . . . . . . . . . . . . . . . . . . . . . . . . 20

## Dust particles                                          21

The emptiness of a composition of dust particles . . . . . . . .  21

The fundamental absence of a composition of dust particles . .  22

The emptiness of the smallest entity . . . . . . . . . . . . . .  22

## Form                                                    23

The emptiness of form . . . . . . . . . . . . . . . . . . . . . .  23

The fundamental absence of form . . . . . . . . . . . . . . . .  23

## The true nature of all                                  24

Empty and fundamentally absent . . . . . . . . . . . . . . . .  24

The emptiness of entities . . . . . . . . . . . . . . . . . . . .  24

The fundamental absence of entities . . . . . . . . . . . . . .  24

The true nature of all . . . . . . . . . . . . . . . . . . . . . .  24

The true nature of all . . . . . . . . . . . . . . . . . . . . . .  24

Perception . . . . . . . . . . . . . . . . . . . . . . . . . . . .  24

## All is mind                                             25

The notion of an entity . . . . . . . . . . . . . . . . . . . . .  25

The notion of inherent existence . . . . . . . . . . . . . . . .  25

Forests, mountains, and rivers . . . . . . . . . . . . . . . . .  26

## Perception                                              28

The perception of entities . . . . . . . . . . . . . . . . . . .  28

The perception of inherent existence . . . . . . . . . . . . . .  28

Illusion . . . . . . . . . . . . . . . . . . . . . . . . . . . . .  29

Forests, mountains, and rivers . . . . . . . . . . . . . . . . .  29

## Inherently existent entities                            31

Inherently existent entities . . . . . . . . . . . . . . . . . . .  31

Forests, mountains, and rivers . . . . . . . . . . . . . . . . .  31

## The emptiness of a world                                33

A world . . . . . . . . . . . . . . . . . . . . . . . . . . . . .  33

The emptiness of a world . . . . . . . . . . . . . . . . . . . .  33

The emptiness of a world . . . . . . . . . . . . . . . . . . . .  33

The fundamental absence of a world . . . . . . . . . . . . . . . 34

The fundamental absence of a world . . . . . . . . . . . . . . 34

The fundamental absence of a world . . . . . . . . . . . . . . 35

The notion of a world . . . . . . . . . . . . . . . . . . . . . . 35

The notion of inherent existence . . . . . . . . . . . . . . . . 36

An inherently existent world . . . . . . . . . . . . . . . . . . 36

Perception . . . . . . . . . . . . . . . . . . . . . . . . . . . . 36

A mass of dust particles . . . . . . . . . . . . . . . . . . . . 37

**Two notions**                                                    **38**

Thinking . . . . . . . . . . . . . . . . . . . . . . . . . . . . 38

Formation and cessation . . . . . . . . . . . . . . . . . . . . 38

Two notions . . . . . . . . . . . . . . . . . . . . . . . . . . . 39

Habit of mind . . . . . . . . . . . . . . . . . . . . . . . . . . 39

Quickness . . . . . . . . . . . . . . . . . . . . . . . . . . . . 39

Fierceness . . . . . . . . . . . . . . . . . . . . . . . . . . . . 40

A continuation of notions . . . . . . . . . . . . . . . . . . . 40

Constant presence . . . . . . . . . . . . . . . . . . . . . . . 41

**Revealing the true nature of all**                               **42**

The fundamental absence of entities . . . . . . . . . . . . . . 42

The emptiness of entities . . . . . . . . . . . . . . . . . . . . 42

Forests, mountains, and rivers . . . . . . . . . . . . . . . . . 43

**Revealing the true nature of all**                               **45**

The emptiness and fundamental absence of entities . . . . . . . 45

The true nature of all . . . . . . . . . . . . . . . . . . . . . . 45

Forests, mountains, and rivers . . . . . . . . . . . . . . . . . 46

**Detachment**                                                     **48**

Revealing the true nature of all . . . . . . . . . . . . . . . . 48

Detachment from the notion of an entity . . . . . . . . . . . . 48

Detachment from the notion of inherent existence . . . . . . . 48

Discontinue the formation . . . . . . . . . . . . . . . . . . . 49

Discontinue the formation . . . . . . . . . . . . . . . . . . . 49

Seek the immediate absence . . . . . . . . . . . . . . . . . . . . 50

Seek the immediate absence . . . . . . . . . . . . . . . . . . . . 50

Withstand the fierceness . . . . . . . . . . . . . . . . . . . . . 50

Withstand the fierceness . . . . . . . . . . . . . . . . . . . . . 51

A continuation of notions . . . . . . . . . . . . . . . . . . . . 51

A continuation of notions . . . . . . . . . . . . . . . . . . . . 51

Endurance . . . . . . . . . . . . . . . . . . . . . . . . . . . . . 52

Endurance . . . . . . . . . . . . . . . . . . . . . . . . . . . . . 52

Two notions . . . . . . . . . . . . . . . . . . . . . . . . . . . . 53

Two notions . . . . . . . . . . . . . . . . . . . . . . . . . . . . 53

Cease the coming together . . . . . . . . . . . . . . . . . . . . 54

Cease the coming together . . . . . . . . . . . . . . . . . . . . 54

The meaning of all buddhas . . . . . . . . . . . . . . . . . . . 55

## Detachment      56

Forests, mountains, and rivers . . . . . . . . . . . . . . . . . . 56

## Detachment in the dust of form      58

Detachment from the notion of an entity . . . . . . . . . . . . 58

One and the same . . . . . . . . . . . . . . . . . . . . . . . . 58

Detachment from the notion of inherent existence . . . . . . . 59

One and the same . . . . . . . . . . . . . . . . . . . . . . . . 59

Forests, mountains, and rivers . . . . . . . . . . . . . . . . . . 60

## The emptiness of a tree and garden      63

The emptiness of a tree . . . . . . . . . . . . . . . . . . . . . 63

The emptiness of a garden . . . . . . . . . . . . . . . . . . . . 66

## Detachment in the five dusts      69

Detachment in the dust of form . . . . . . . . . . . . . . . . . 69

Detachment in the dust of sound . . . . . . . . . . . . . . . . 69

Detachment in the dust of smell . . . . . . . . . . . . . . . . . 70

Detachment in the dust of taste . . . . . . . . . . . . . . . . . 70

Detachment in the dust of touch . . . . . . . . . . . . . . . . . 71

**The three essentials**     **72**

Detachment . . . . . . . . . . . . . . . . . . . . . . . . . . . . . 72

The three essentials . . . . . . . . . . . . . . . . . . . . . . . 72

The three essentials . . . . . . . . . . . . . . . . . . . . . . . 73

**Mindfulness**     **74**

Mindfulness . . . . . . . . . . . . . . . . . . . . . . . . . . . . 74

Sitting meditation . . . . . . . . . . . . . . . . . . . . . . . . 74

Mindfulness of the Buddha . . . . . . . . . . . . . . . . . . 75

Wandering thoughts . . . . . . . . . . . . . . . . . . . . . . . 76

One notion at a time . . . . . . . . . . . . . . . . . . . . . . . 76

Taming the mind . . . . . . . . . . . . . . . . . . . . . . . . . 77

Stilling the mind . . . . . . . . . . . . . . . . . . . . . . . . . 77

Walking, standing, sitting, and lying down . . . . . . . . . . . 78

Walking meditation . . . . . . . . . . . . . . . . . . . . . . . 78

Walking meditation . . . . . . . . . . . . . . . . . . . . . . . 79

In stillness and in motion . . . . . . . . . . . . . . . . . . . . 80

Feelings . . . . . . . . . . . . . . . . . . . . . . . . . . . . . . 80

Vexation . . . . . . . . . . . . . . . . . . . . . . . . . . . . . . 81

**Awareness and endurance: Notion of an entity**     **82**

Awareness . . . . . . . . . . . . . . . . . . . . . . . . . . . . . 82

Awareness . . . . . . . . . . . . . . . . . . . . . . . . . . . . . 82

Endurance . . . . . . . . . . . . . . . . . . . . . . . . . . . . . 83

Mindfulness, awareness, and endurance . . . . . . . . . . . . 83

**Awareness and endurance: Notion of inherent existence**     **84**

Awareness . . . . . . . . . . . . . . . . . . . . . . . . . . . . . 84

Awareness . . . . . . . . . . . . . . . . . . . . . . . . . . . . . 84

Endurance . . . . . . . . . . . . . . . . . . . . . . . . . . . . . 85

Mindfulness, awareness, and endurance . . . . . . . . . . . . 85

**The three essentials**     **86**

Cultivation . . . . . . . . . . . . . . . . . . . . . . . . . . . . 86

Meditation . . . . . . . . . . . . . . . . . . . . . . . . . . . . 86

In stillness and in motion . . . . . . . . . . . . . . . . . . . 87

**The ability to withstand** **88**

The impenetrableness of notions of entities . . . . . . . . . . . 88

The impenetrableness of the notion of inherent existence . . . . 88

Heaven and earth . . . . . . . . . . . . . . . . . . . . . . . . 89

Feelings . . . . . . . . . . . . . . . . . . . . . . . . . . . . . 89

In stillness and in motion . . . . . . . . . . . . . . . . . . . 90

Breaking through . . . . . . . . . . . . . . . . . . . . . . . . 90

**The perfection of wisdom** **91**

Detachment from all notions of entities . . . . . . . . . . . . . 91

Detachment from the notion of inherent existence . . . . . . . . 91

**Ignorance and wisdom** **92**

Suffering . . . . . . . . . . . . . . . . . . . . . . . . . . . . . 92

Ignorance . . . . . . . . . . . . . . . . . . . . . . . . . . . . . 92

Cessation of ignorance . . . . . . . . . . . . . . . . . . . . . . 92

Detachment . . . . . . . . . . . . . . . . . . . . . . . . . . . . 93

The perfection of wisdom . . . . . . . . . . . . . . . . . . . . 93

**The emptiness of the self** **94**

The self . . . . . . . . . . . . . . . . . . . . . . . . . . . . . . 94

The emptiness of the self . . . . . . . . . . . . . . . . . . . . 94

The emptiness of the self . . . . . . . . . . . . . . . . . . . . 94

The fundamental absence of the self . . . . . . . . . . . . . . . 95

The fundamental absence of the self . . . . . . . . . . . . . . . 95

The fundamental absence of the self . . . . . . . . . . . . . . . 96

The notion of self . . . . . . . . . . . . . . . . . . . . . . . . 96

The notion of inherent existence . . . . . . . . . . . . . . . . . 96

An inherently existent self . . . . . . . . . . . . . . . . . . . . 97

Perception . . . . . . . . . . . . . . . . . . . . . . . . . . . . . 97

Revealing the fundamental absence of the self . . . . . . . . . . 98

Revealing the emptiness of the self . . . . . . . . . . . . . . . 98

Revealing the true nature of the self . . . . . . . . . . . . . . . 99

Detachment from the notion of self . . . . . . . . . . . . . . . 99

Detachment from the notion of inherent existence . . . . . . . . 100

The perfection of wisdom . . . . . . . . . . . . . . . . . . . 100

## Detachment from the notion of self         101

The three essentials . . . . . . . . . . . . . . . . . . . . . 101

Mindfulness . . . . . . . . . . . . . . . . . . . . . . . . . 101

Awareness . . . . . . . . . . . . . . . . . . . . . . . . . . 101

Awareness . . . . . . . . . . . . . . . . . . . . . . . . . . 102

Awareness . . . . . . . . . . . . . . . . . . . . . . . . . . 102

Endurance . . . . . . . . . . . . . . . . . . . . . . . . . . 102

In stillness and in motion . . . . . . . . . . . . . . . . . . 103

The emptiness of the self . . . . . . . . . . . . . . . . . . 103

## The emptiness of a person         104

A person . . . . . . . . . . . . . . . . . . . . . . . . . . . 104

The emptiness of a person . . . . . . . . . . . . . . . . . . 104

The emptiness of a person . . . . . . . . . . . . . . . . . . 104

The fundamental absence of a person . . . . . . . . . . . . . 105

The fundamental absence of a person . . . . . . . . . . . . . 105

The fundamental absence of a person . . . . . . . . . . . . . 106

The notion of a person . . . . . . . . . . . . . . . . . . . . 106

The notion of inherent existence . . . . . . . . . . . . . . . 106

An inherently existent person . . . . . . . . . . . . . . . . 107

Perception . . . . . . . . . . . . . . . . . . . . . . . . . . 107

Revealing the fundamental absence of a person . . . . . . . . 108

Revealing the emptiness of a person . . . . . . . . . . . . . 108

Revealing the true nature of a person . . . . . . . . . . . . 109

Detachment from the notion of a person . . . . . . . . . . . 109

Detachment from the notion of inherent existence . . . . . . . 110

The perfection of wisdom . . . . . . . . . . . . . . . . . . . 110

**Detachment from the notion of a person**     **111**

The three essentials . . . . . . . . . . . . . . . . . . . . . . 111

Mindfulness . . . . . . . . . . . . . . . . . . . . . . . . . . . 111

Awareness . . . . . . . . . . . . . . . . . . . . . . . . . . . . 111

Awareness . . . . . . . . . . . . . . . . . . . . . . . . . . . . 112

Endurance . . . . . . . . . . . . . . . . . . . . . . . . . . . . 112

In stillness and in motion . . . . . . . . . . . . . . . . . . . 113

The emptiness of a person . . . . . . . . . . . . . . . . . . . 113

**Detachment from the notion of a person**     **114**

Form is devoid of a person . . . . . . . . . . . . . . . . . . . 114

Sound is devoid of a person . . . . . . . . . . . . . . . . . . 115

**The emptiness of the body**     **116**

The body . . . . . . . . . . . . . . . . . . . . . . . . . . . . 116

The emptiness of the body . . . . . . . . . . . . . . . . . . . 116

The fundamental absence of the body . . . . . . . . . . . . . 116

The fundamental absence of the body . . . . . . . . . . . . . 117

A composition of entities . . . . . . . . . . . . . . . . . . . . 117

The emptiness of the body (i) . . . . . . . . . . . . . . . . . 117

The fundamental absence of the body (i) . . . . . . . . . . . 118

The emptiness of the body (ii) . . . . . . . . . . . . . . . . . 118

The fundamental absence of the body (ii) . . . . . . . . . . . 119

The emptiness of the body (iii) . . . . . . . . . . . . . . . . . 120

The fundamental absence of the body (iii) . . . . . . . . . . . 120

The notion of a body . . . . . . . . . . . . . . . . . . . . . . 121

The notion of inherent existence . . . . . . . . . . . . . . . . 121

An inherently existent body . . . . . . . . . . . . . . . . . . 121

Perception . . . . . . . . . . . . . . . . . . . . . . . . . . . . 122

Revealing the fundamental absence of the body . . . . . . . . 123

Revealing the emptiness of the body . . . . . . . . . . . . . . 123

Revealing the true nature of the body . . . . . . . . . . . . . 124

Detachment from the notion of a body . . . . . . . . . . . . . 124

Detachment from the notion of inherent existence . . . . . . . 125

The perfection of wisdom . . . . . . . . . . . . . . . . . . . . 125

**Detachment from the notion of a body**        **126**

The three essentials . . . . . . . . . . . . . . . . . . . . . . 126

Mindfulness . . . . . . . . . . . . . . . . . . . . . . . . . . . 126

Awareness . . . . . . . . . . . . . . . . . . . . . . . . . . . . 126

Awareness . . . . . . . . . . . . . . . . . . . . . . . . . . . . 127

Endurance . . . . . . . . . . . . . . . . . . . . . . . . . . . . 127

In stillness and in motion . . . . . . . . . . . . . . . . . . . 128

The emptiness of the body . . . . . . . . . . . . . . . . . 128

**Detachment from the notion of a body**        **129**

Form is devoid of a body . . . . . . . . . . . . . . . . . . . 129

**The emptiness of a sentient being**        **130**

The emptiness of a sentient being . . . . . . . . . . . . . . 130

The emptiness of a bodhisattva . . . . . . . . . . . . . . . 133

**Contemplation**        **135**

Elephants . . . . . . . . . . . . . . . . . . . . . . . . . . . . 135

Compositions . . . . . . . . . . . . . . . . . . . . . . . . . . 135

Compositions . . . . . . . . . . . . . . . . . . . . . . . . . . 136

**The emptiness of the five skandhas**        **137**

The emptiness of form . . . . . . . . . . . . . . . . . . . . . 137

The emptiness of feeling . . . . . . . . . . . . . . . . . . . . 139

The emptiness of thinking . . . . . . . . . . . . . . . . . . . 141

The emptiness of volition . . . . . . . . . . . . . . . . . . . 143

The emptiness of consciousness . . . . . . . . . . . . . . . 145

**The emptiness of the eighteen sense realms**        **147**

The emptiness of the first sense . . . . . . . . . . . . . . . 147

The emptiness of the first sense object . . . . . . . . . . . 148

The emptiness of the first sense consciousness . . . . . . . 149

The emptiness of the sixth sense . . . . . . . . . . . . . . . 150

The emptiness of the sixth sense object . . . . . . . . . . . 151

The emptiness of the sixth sense consciousness . . . . . . . 152

**The five skandhas and eighteen sense realms**      **153**

The five skandhas . . . . . . . . . . . . . . . . . . . . . . . . . 153

The eighteen sense realms . . . . . . . . . . . . . . . . . . . 153

**The self is a name**      **154**

The self is a name . . . . . . . . . . . . . . . . . . . . . . . . 154

The self is a composition of names . . . . . . . . . . . . . . 154

The self is a name of names . . . . . . . . . . . . . . . . . . 155

**Detachment from the notion of self**      **156**

Detachment from the notion of self . . . . . . . . . . . . . . 156

Detachment from arbitrary and false names . . . . . . . . . 156

Detachment from the notion of inherent existence . . . . . . 157

**The body is a name**      **159**

The body is a name . . . . . . . . . . . . . . . . . . . . . . . 159

The body is a composition of names . . . . . . . . . . . . . . 159

The body is a name of names . . . . . . . . . . . . . . . . . . 160

**Detachment from the notion of a body**      **161**

Detachment from the notion of a body . . . . . . . . . . . . 161

Detachment from arbitrary and false names . . . . . . . . . 161

Detachment from the notion of inherent existence . . . . . . 162

**The emptiness of a lifespan**      **163**

The emptiness of life . . . . . . . . . . . . . . . . . . . . . . 163

The emptiness of a lifespan . . . . . . . . . . . . . . . . . . 165

The emptiness of a lifespan . . . . . . . . . . . . . . . . . . 167

**Four notions**      **170**

Four notions . . . . . . . . . . . . . . . . . . . . . . . . . . . 170

Unsurpassed complete enlightenment . . . . . . . . . . . . . 170

The notion of self . . . . . . . . . . . . . . . . . . . . . . . . 170

The notion of self . . . . . . . . . . . . . . . . . . . . . . . . 171

The notion of self . . . . . . . . . . . . . . . . . . . . . . . . 172

The notion of a person . . . . . . . . . . . . . . . . . . . . . 173

The notion of a person . . . . . . . . . . . . . . . . . . . . . . . . . 173

The notion of a sentient being . . . . . . . . . . . . . . . . . . 174

The notion of a sentient being . . . . . . . . . . . . . . . . . . 174

The notion of a sentient being . . . . . . . . . . . . . . . . . . 174

The notion of a lifespan . . . . . . . . . . . . . . . . . . . . . . . 175

The notion of a lifespan . . . . . . . . . . . . . . . . . . . . . . . 176

Four names . . . . . . . . . . . . . . . . . . . . . . . . . . . . . . . . 176

**The Diamond Sutra**                                      **177**

Upholding the Diamond Sutra . . . . . . . . . . . . . . . . . 177

Diamond wisdom . . . . . . . . . . . . . . . . . . . . . . . . . . . 177

Unsurpassed complete enlightenment . . . . . . . . . . . . . 178

**Virtue**                                                 **179**

Virtue . . . . . . . . . . . . . . . . . . . . . . . . . . . . . . . . . . . 179

The five precepts . . . . . . . . . . . . . . . . . . . . . . . . . . . 179

The ten virtues . . . . . . . . . . . . . . . . . . . . . . . . . . . . 179

The six perfections . . . . . . . . . . . . . . . . . . . . . . . . . . 179

The perfection of wisdom . . . . . . . . . . . . . . . . . . . . . 180

Virtue and wisdom . . . . . . . . . . . . . . . . . . . . . . . . . . 180

Giving and wisdom . . . . . . . . . . . . . . . . . . . . . . . . . . 180

Giving and wisdom . . . . . . . . . . . . . . . . . . . . . . . . . . 181

Giving and wisdom . . . . . . . . . . . . . . . . . . . . . . . . . . 181

Giving and wisdom . . . . . . . . . . . . . . . . . . . . . . . . . . 182

Giving and wisdom . . . . . . . . . . . . . . . . . . . . . . . . . . 182

**Emptiness**                                              **184**

Emptiness . . . . . . . . . . . . . . . . . . . . . . . . . . . . . . . . 184

Understanding . . . . . . . . . . . . . . . . . . . . . . . . . . . . . 185

The notion of inherent existence . . . . . . . . . . . . . . . . 185

Perception . . . . . . . . . . . . . . . . . . . . . . . . . . . . . . . . 185

In emptiness . . . . . . . . . . . . . . . . . . . . . . . . . . . . . . 186

**People**                    **187**

The perception of people . . . . . . . . . . . . . . . . . . . . . . 187

The fundamental absence of people . . . . . . . . . . . . . . . 187

All is devoid of people . . . . . . . . . . . . . . . . . . . . . . . 187

The notion of people . . . . . . . . . . . . . . . . . . . . . . . . 187

**Desire and hatred**        **188**

The cause of suffering . . . . . . . . . . . . . . . . . . . . . . . 188

Desire . . . . . . . . . . . . . . . . . . . . . . . . . . . . . . . . . 188

Hatred . . . . . . . . . . . . . . . . . . . . . . . . . . . . . . . . . 188

Ignorance . . . . . . . . . . . . . . . . . . . . . . . . . . . . . . . 189

Wisdom . . . . . . . . . . . . . . . . . . . . . . . . . . . . . . . . 189

The cessation of the afflictions . . . . . . . . . . . . . . . . . 189

**Desire and lust**        **190**

Desire and lust . . . . . . . . . . . . . . . . . . . . . . . . . . . . 190

Worldly dusts . . . . . . . . . . . . . . . . . . . . . . . . . . . . . 190

Detachment from desire and lust . . . . . . . . . . . . . . . . 191

Mindfulness, awareness, and endurance . . . . . . . . . . . . . 191

Mindfulness of the Buddha . . . . . . . . . . . . . . . . . . . . 191

Lascivious thoughts . . . . . . . . . . . . . . . . . . . . . . . . . 191

Detachment from the notion of self, a person, and a body . . . 192

Detachment from the notion of inherent existence . . . . . . . . 193

**Anger and hatred**        **194**

Anger and hatred . . . . . . . . . . . . . . . . . . . . . . . . . . 194

Detachment from anger and hatred . . . . . . . . . . . . . . . 194

Mindfulness, awareness, and endurance . . . . . . . . . . . . . 194

Mindfulness of the Buddha . . . . . . . . . . . . . . . . . . . . 195

Detachment from notions of entities . . . . . . . . . . . . . . 195

Detachment from the notion of inherent existence . . . . . . . . 196

## Arrogance                                                                197

Arrogance . . . . . . . . . . . . . . . . . . . . . . . . . . . . . . . . . 197

The fierceness of the notion of self . . . . . . . . . . . . . . . 197

Detachment from arrogance . . . . . . . . . . . . . . . . . . . . 198

Mindfulness, awareness, and endurance . . . . . . . . . . . . . 198

Detachment from the notion of self and others . . . . . . . . 198

Detachment from the notion of inherent existence . . . . . . . 199

Severe flaw . . . . . . . . . . . . . . . . . . . . . . . . . . . . . . 200

Grave fault . . . . . . . . . . . . . . . . . . . . . . . . . . . . . . 200

## The emptiness of motion and positions                                    201

The emptiness of the motion of walking . . . . . . . . . . . . 201

The emptiness of the position of standing . . . . . . . . . . . 204

Motions and positions . . . . . . . . . . . . . . . . . . . . . . . 206

Gestures and expressions . . . . . . . . . . . . . . . . . . . . . 207

## The emptiness of a quality and circumstance                              208

The emptiness of a quality . . . . . . . . . . . . . . . . . . . . 208

The emptiness of a circumstance . . . . . . . . . . . . . . . . . 209

## The emptiness of the mind and notions                                    211

The emptiness of the mind . . . . . . . . . . . . . . . . . . . . 211

The emptiness of thoughts . . . . . . . . . . . . . . . . . . . . . 213

The emptiness of the notion of self . . . . . . . . . . . . . . . 215

The notion of self . . . . . . . . . . . . . . . . . . . . . . . . . . 216

## Grasping at emptiness                                                    217

Emptiness . . . . . . . . . . . . . . . . . . . . . . . . . . . . . . 217

The thought of the emptiness of an entity . . . . . . . . . . . 217

The thought of the absence of inherent existence . . . . . . . 217

Detachment . . . . . . . . . . . . . . . . . . . . . . . . . . . . . 217

## Grasping at the absence of entities                                      218

The thought of the absence of an entity . . . . . . . . . . . . 218

The thought of the absence of the self . . . . . . . . . . . . . 218

The thought of the absence of people . . . . . . . . . . . . . . 218

In emptiness . . . . . . . . . . . . . . . . . . . . . . . . . . . . 218

**Detachment in the sixth dust**          **219**
Detachment in the presence of thoughts . . . . . . . . . . . . 219

**Mindfulness of sound and form**          **221**
Mindfulness of sound . . . . . . . . . . . . . . . . . . . . . . . 221
Mindfulness of form . . . . . . . . . . . . . . . . . . . . . . . . 222

**Mindfulness and endurance**          **223**
Notions of entities . . . . . . . . . . . . . . . . . . . . . . . . . 223
The notion of inherent existence . . . . . . . . . . . . . . . . . 223

**The notion of inherent existence**          **224**
Awareness . . . . . . . . . . . . . . . . . . . . . . . . . . . . . . 224
A feeling of presence . . . . . . . . . . . . . . . . . . . . . . . . 224
Space in the east . . . . . . . . . . . . . . . . . . . . . . . . . . 225
Flower in the sky . . . . . . . . . . . . . . . . . . . . . . . . . . 225

**Habit of mind**          **226**
The notion of an entity . . . . . . . . . . . . . . . . . . . . . . 226
The self, people, and the body . . . . . . . . . . . . . . . . . . 226
The notion of inherent existence . . . . . . . . . . . . . . . . . 227

**Detachment**          **228**
Notions of entities . . . . . . . . . . . . . . . . . . . . . . . . . 228
The notion of a large entity . . . . . . . . . . . . . . . . . . . . 228
Complete scenery . . . . . . . . . . . . . . . . . . . . . . . . . . 229
Sword of wisdom . . . . . . . . . . . . . . . . . . . . . . . . . . 229

**Subjugating the mind**          **230**
Feelings . . . . . . . . . . . . . . . . . . . . . . . . . . . . . . . 230
Perception . . . . . . . . . . . . . . . . . . . . . . . . . . . . . . 230

**Vigor**          **231**
The notion of self and people . . . . . . . . . . . . . . . . . . . 231
The notion of inherent existence . . . . . . . . . . . . . . . . . 231

**Sovereignty**      **232**

The perfection of meditation . . . . . . . . . . . . . . . . . . 232

Sovereignty . . . . . . . . . . . . . . . . . . . . . . . . . . . 232

Sovereignty . . . . . . . . . . . . . . . . . . . . . . . . . . . 232

Sovereignty . . . . . . . . . . . . . . . . . . . . . . . . . . . 233

The perfection of meditation . . . . . . . . . . . . . . . . . . 233

**The true nature of all**      **234**

All is devoid of a self . . . . . . . . . . . . . . . . . . . . . 234

All is devoid of inherent existence . . . . . . . . . . . . . . . 234

**Investigating the origin of words**      **235**

Who is mindful of the Buddha? . . . . . . . . . . . . . . . . . 235

**Detachment in the presence of sound**      **236**

Notions of entities . . . . . . . . . . . . . . . . . . . . . . . 236

The notion of self . . . . . . . . . . . . . . . . . . . . . . . 236

The notion of people . . . . . . . . . . . . . . . . . . . . . . 237

The notion of inherent existence . . . . . . . . . . . . . . . . 237

**Detachment in the presence of form**      **238**

Notions of entities . . . . . . . . . . . . . . . . . . . . . . . 238

The notion of self . . . . . . . . . . . . . . . . . . . . . . . 238

The notion of people . . . . . . . . . . . . . . . . . . . . . . 239

The notion of a body . . . . . . . . . . . . . . . . . . . . . . 239

The notion of inherent existence . . . . . . . . . . . . . . . . 240

**Detachment in the presence of touch**      **241**

The notion of a body . . . . . . . . . . . . . . . . . . . . . . 241

The notion of inherent existence . . . . . . . . . . . . . . . . 241

**Detachment in the presence of thoughts**      **242**

Notions of entities . . . . . . . . . . . . . . . . . . . . . . . 242

The notion of self . . . . . . . . . . . . . . . . . . . . . . . 242

The notion of inherent existence . . . . . . . . . . . . . . . . 243

**Bodhisattva**      **244**

The resolve to attain enlightenment . . . . . . . . . . . . . . 244

The bodhisattva way . . . . . . . . . . . . . . . . . . . . . . 244

**The self, a person, and the body**      **245**

The emptiness of the self . . . . . . . . . . . . . . . . . . . 245

The emptiness of a person . . . . . . . . . . . . . . . . . . . 246

The emptiness of the body . . . . . . . . . . . . . . . . . . . 247

**The meaning of the way**      **248**

The cessation of the mind . . . . . . . . . . . . . . . . . . . 248

The notion of self . . . . . . . . . . . . . . . . . . . . . . . 248

The meaning of the way . . . . . . . . . . . . . . . . . . . . 248

# Emptiness

# Unsurpassed complete enlightenment

### Suffering

Samsara is endless suffering. Samsara is the endless cycle of birth and death. Sentient beings wander in samsara since time without beginning. Sentient beings suffer in samsara since time without beginning. Suffering has a cause. The afflictions are the cause of suffering. The afflictions are ignorance, desire, and hatred. Suffering can be ceased. Suffering can be ceased by ceasing the cause of suffering. Suffering can be ceased by ceasing ignorance, desire, and hatred. The cessation of the afflictions is the cessation of suffering. The cessation of the afflictions is nirvana. Nirvana is liberation from suffering. Nirvana is liberation from samsara.

### The end of ignorance

Ignorance, desire, and hatred are the cause of suffering. Desire and hatred arise from ignorance. Ignorance is the fundamental cause of suffering. Suffering can be ceased by ceasing the cause of suffering. Suffering can be ceased by ceasing the affliction of ignorance. The end of ignorance is the end of suffering. The end of ignorance is unsurpassed complete enlightenment. Unsurpassed complete enlightenment is the end of suffering. All sentient beings can attain unsurpassed complete enlightenment by upholding the teaching of the Buddha. All sentient beings can attain unsurpassed complete enlightenment by cultivating the bodhisattva way.

### Unsurpassed complete enlightenment

Unsurpassed complete enlightenment is the end of ignorance. The term 'unsurpassed complete enlightenment' is derived from the Sanskrit term 'anuttara-samyak-sambodhi'. 'Anuttara' means 'highest' or 'unsurpassed'. 'Bodhi' means 'awakening' or 'enlightenment'. 'Samyak-sambodhi' means 'right and complete enlightenment'. 'Anuttara-samyak-sambodhi' means 'unsurpassed complete enlightenment'.

1

The mind that has attained unsurpassed complete enlightenment is a buddha. 'Buddha' is Sanskrit and means 'awakened' or 'enlightened'. The mind that is cultivating the way and that has not yet attained enlightenment is a bodhisattva. 'Bodhi' means 'awakening' or 'enlightenment'. 'Sattva' is Sanskrit and means 'sentient being'. A bodhisattva is a sentient being that enlightens all sentient beings.

### The resolve to attain enlightenment

Unsurpassed complete enlightenment arises from the resolve to attain unsurpassed complete enlightenment. The resolve to attain unsurpassed complete enlightenment is the seed. Unsurpassed complete enlightenment is the fruit. To resolve to attain unsurpassed complete enlightenment is to declare, "I resolve to attain unsurpassed complete enlightenment." To resolve to attain unsurpassed complete enlightenment is to cultivate the bodhisattva way. The resolve to attain enlightenment is the beginning of the end of suffering.

### The bodhisattva way

To resolve to attain unsurpassed complete enlightenment is to cultivate the bodhisattva way. To cultivate the bodhisattva way is to vow to liberate all sentient beings from samsara by leading them to nirvana. To cultivate the bodhisattva way is to vow to remain involved in samsara for all time until all sentient beings are liberated. To cultivate the bodhisattva way is to benefit and enlighten self and others. To cultivate the bodhisattva way is to cultivate the six perfections. To cultivate the bodhisattva way is to cultivate compassion and wisdom. To cultivate the bodhisattva way is to cultivate virtue and wisdom.

### The six perfections

Unsurpassed complete enlightenment is attained by cultivating the six perfections. The six perfections are the perfection of giving, discipline, endurance, vigor, meditation, and wisdom. The term 'perfection' is derived from the Sanskrit term 'paramita'. 'Paramita' means 'beyond to the other shore'. To go beyond is to go beyond from this shore to the other shore. 'This shore' is ignorance and samsara. 'The other shore' is enlightenment and nirvana. By cultivating the six perfections, sentient beings go beyond ignorance and suffering and arrive at unsurpassed complete enlightenment and the end of suffering.

### The perfection of giving

The perfection of giving is the cultivation of benevolent giving. To cultivate giving is to give and provide offerings. To cultivate giving is to give and provide the teaching of the Buddha. To cultivate giving is to give and provide fearlessness to those who are fearful. Giving is the absence of greed.

### The perfection of discipline

The perfection of discipline is the cultivation of moral discipline. To cultivate discipline is to uphold and observe precepts. The upholding of precepts such as the five precepts is the foundation of the way. The five precepts are the abstention from killing, stealing, sexual misconduct, lying, and intoxication. Discipline is the absence of evil.

### The perfection of endurance

The perfection of endurance is the cultivation of patient endurance. To cultivate endurance is to endure patiently the absence of anger and hatred. To cultivate endurance is to exercise tolerance and patience in the presence of adversity and hardship. Endurance is the absence of anger.

### The perfection of vigor

The perfection of vigor is the cultivation of vigor. To cultivate vigor is to resolve to accomplish and succeed in virtuous endeavors. To cultivate vigor is to persevere in and to not retreat from virtuous endeavors. To refrain from indolence is to cultivate vigor. Vigor is the absence of indolence.

### The perfection of meditation

The perfection of meditation is the cultivation of meditation. To cultivate meditation is to detach from delusive notions that arise from the mind. To cultivate meditation is to attain sovereignty over delusive notions that arise from the mind. The absence of delusive notions is the presence of mindfulness. Meditation is the presence of mindfulness.

### The perfection of wisdom

The perfection of wisdom is the cultivation of wisdom. To cultivate wisdom is to see and understand the true nature of all. Emptiness is the true nature of all. The emptiness of entities is the absence of inherent existence entities are perceived to be endowed with. Wisdom is the absence of ignorance.

### The other shore

The six perfections are the perfection of giving, discipline, endurance, vigor, meditation, and wisdom. Unsurpassed complete enlightenment is attained by cultivating the six perfections. Unsurpassed complete enlightenment is attained by cultivating the perfection of wisdom. Wisdom is the absence of ignorance. Enlightenment is the end of ignorance. The end of ignorance is the end of suffering. The end of ignorance is the other shore.

## The bodhisattva way

A bodhisattva cultivates the bodhisattva way. A buddha has completed the bodhisattva way. A bodhisattva cultivates compassion and wisdom. A buddha has perfected compassion and wisdom. A bodhisattva cultivates virtue and wisdom. A buddha has perfected merit and wisdom. A bodhisattva cultivates the six perfections. A buddha has completed the six perfections. A bodhisattva cultivates the perfection of wisdom. A buddha has completed the perfection of wisdom. A bodhisattva resolves to attain unsurpassed complete enlightenment. A buddha has attained unsurpassed complete enlightenment.

# The five skandhas and eighteen sense realms

### The five skandhas

All existence arises from the five skandhas. The five skandhas are form, feeling, thinking, volition, and consciousness.

### The eighteen sense realms

All is perceived by way of the eighteen sense realms. The eighteen sense realms are the six senses, the six sense objects, and the six sense consciousnesses. The six senses are the eyes, the ears, the nose, the tongue, the body, and the mind. The six sense objects are form, sound, smell, taste, touch, and notions. The six sense objects are also known as the six dusts. The six sense consciousnesses are the consciousness of the eyes, the consciousness of the ears, the consciousness of the nose, the consciousness of the tongue, the consciousness of the body, and the consciousness of the mind.

### The eighteen sense realms

Seeing is the coming together of the eyes, form, and the consciousness of the eyes. Hearing is the coming together of the ears, sound, and the consciousness of the ears. Smelling is the coming together of the nose, smell, and the consciousness of the nose. Tasting is the coming together of the tongue, taste, and the consciousness of the tongue. Feeling is the coming together of the body, touch, and the consciousness of the body. Thinking and feeling are the coming together of the mind, notions, and the consciousness of the mind.

# Inherent existence

### Entities

The mind perceives the presence of entities. The mind is that which is aware and present. An entity is that which is perceived by the mind.

### Inherent existence

The mind perceives the presence of entities. Entities perceived by the mind are perceived to be endowed with inherent existence.

### Inherent existence

Inherent existence is a quality of entities. Inherent existence is independent existence. To be endowed with inherent existence is to exist independently. To be endowed with inherent existence is to exist by itself and in itself. That which exists independently is an entity. That which is endowed with inherent existence is an entity. An entity is an entity endowed with inherent existence. An entity is an inherently existent entity.

### Endowed with inherent existence

To perceive an entity to be endowed with inherent existence is to perceive an entity to exist independently from everything else. To perceive an entity to exist independently from everything else is to perceive an entity to be endowed with inherent existence.

### Endowed with inherent existence

To perceive an entity to be endowed with inherent existence is to perceive an entity to exist by itself and in itself. To perceive an entity to exist by itself and in itself is to perceive an entity to be endowed with inherent existence.

### Endowed with inherent existence

To perceive an entity to be endowed with inherent existence is to perceive an entity as a separate and distinct entity. To perceive an entity as a separate and distinct entity is to perceive an entity to be endowed with inherent existence.


### Perception

Entities are perceived to be endowed with inherent existence. That which perceives is the mind. That which is perceived is inherent existence. The mind perceives the presence of inherent existence.


### Inseparable

Inherent existence is that which indwells in an entity. An entity is that which is endowed with inherent existence. An entity and the inherent existence indwelling in an entity are inseparable.


### Inseparable

An entity is an entity endowed with inherent existence. An entity endowed with inherent existence is an entity. An entity and the inherent existence indwelling in an entity are inseparable.


### Inseparable

The presence of an entity is the presence of inherent existence indwelling in an entity. The presence of inherent existence indwelling in an entity is the presence of an entity. An entity and the inherent existence indwelling in an entity are inseparable.

### Independently existent entities

An independently existent entity is an entity endowed with inherent existence. An entity endowed with inherent existence is an independently existent entity.

The presence of an independently existent entity is the presence of inherent existence. The perception of an independently existent entity is the perception of inherent existence.

### Separate and distinct entities

A separate and distinct entity is an entity endowed with inherent existence. An entity endowed with inherent existence is a separate and distinct entity.

The presence of a separate and distinct entity is the presence of inherent existence. The perception of a separate and distinct entity is the perception of inherent existence.

### Entities

An entity is an entity endowed with inherent existence. An entity endowed with inherent existence is an entity.

The presence of an entity is the presence of inherent existence. The perception of an entity is the perception of inherent existence.

### Entities

An entity is that which is perceived to be endowed with inherent existence. That which is perceived to be endowed with inherent existence is an entity.

**Forest**

The mind perceives the presence of entities. The mind perceives the presence of a forest. A forest is an entity. A forest is perceived to be endowed with inherent existence. To perceive a forest to be endowed with inherent existence is to perceive a forest to exist independently from everything else. To perceive a forest to be endowed with inherent existence is to perceive a forest as a separate and distinct entity. A forest is a forest endowed with inherent existence. A forest and the inherent existence indwelling in a forest are inseparable.

**Mountain**

The mind perceives the presence of entities. The mind perceives the presence of a mountain. A mountain is an entity. A mountain is perceived to be endowed with inherent existence. To perceive a mountain to be endowed with inherent existence is to perceive a mountain to exist independently from everything else. To perceive a mountain to be endowed with inherent existence is to perceive a mountain as a separate and distinct entity. A mountain is a mountain endowed with inherent existence. A mountain and the inherent existence indwelling in a mountain are inseparable.

**River**

The mind perceives the presence of entities. The mind perceives the presence of a river. A river is an entity. A river is perceived to be endowed with inherent existence. To perceive a river to be endowed with inherent existence is to perceive a river to exist independently from everything else. To perceive a river to be endowed with inherent existence is to perceive a river as a separate and distinct entity. A river is a river endowed with inherent existence. A river and the inherent existence indwelling in a river are inseparable.

# The emptiness of entities

### All is empty

The Buddha teaches that all is empty. The Buddha teaches that all is devoid of inherent existence.

### The emptiness of entities

All is empty. All is devoid of inherent existence. To be empty is to be devoid of inherent existence. Emptiness is the absence of inherent existence. Emptiness is the absence of the perception of inherent existence.

### The emptiness of entities

Emptiness is a quality of entities. The absence of inherent existence is a quality of entities. To be empty is to not be endowed with inherent existence. To be empty is to be devoid of inherent existence. That which is empty is an entity. That which is devoid of inherent existence is an entity. An entity is an entity devoid of inherent existence.

### The emptiness of entities

Entities are perceived to be endowed with inherent existence. Emptiness is the absence of the perception of inherent existence. The emptiness of entities is the absence of inherent existence entities are perceived to be endowed with.

### The true nature of all

Emptiness is the true nature of all. The absence of inherent existence is the true nature of all. All is devoid of inherent existence. Inherent existence is fundamentally absent.

### Devoid of inherent existence

To perceive an entity to be devoid of inherent existence is to not perceive an entity to exist independently from everything else. To not perceive an entity to exist independently from everything else is to perceive an entity to be devoid of inherent existence.

### Devoid of inherent existence

To perceive an entity to be devoid of inherent existence is to not perceive an entity to exist by itself and in itself. To not perceive an entity to exist by itself and in itself is to perceive an entity to be devoid of inherent existence.

### Devoid of inherent existence

To perceive an entity to be devoid of inherent existence is to not perceive an entity as a separate and distinct entity. To not perceive an entity as a separate and distinct entity is to perceive an entity to be devoid of inherent existence.

### Perception

The Buddha teaches that all is devoid of inherent existence. The mind, however, perceives all to be endowed with inherent existence.

# The emptiness of compositions

## The emptiness of compositions

The Buddha teaches that all is empty. The Buddha teaches that all is devoid of inherent existence. Compositions are empty. Compositions are devoid of inherent existence. A composition is an entity composed of smaller entities. A composition is a composition of smaller entities. That which is composed of smaller entities is dependent on smaller entities. That which is dependent on smaller entities cannot exist independently from smaller entities. That which cannot exist independently from smaller entities cannot exist independently from everything else. That which cannot exist independently from everything else cannot be endowed with inherent existence. That which cannot be endowed with inherent existence is devoid of inherent existence. That which is devoid of inherent existence is empty. A composition is devoid of inherent existence. A composition is empty. The emptiness of a composition is the absence of inherent existence a composition is perceived to be endowed with. That which is composed is inevitably empty. All compositions are empty. All compositions are devoid of inherent existence. To understand that compositions cannot be endowed with inherent existence is to understand the impossibility of compositions to be endowed with inherent existence. To understand that compositions cannot be endowed with inherent existence is to understand conceptually the emptiness of compositions.

## Forest

A forest is empty. A forest is a composition of trees. That which is composed of trees is dependent on trees. That which is dependent on trees cannot exist independently from trees. That which cannot exist independently from trees cannot exist independently from everything else. That which cannot exist independently from everything else cannot be endowed with inherent existence. That which cannot be endowed with inherent existence is devoid of inherent existence. That which is devoid of inherent existence is empty. A forest is devoid of inherent existence. A forest is empty. The emptiness of a forest is the absence of inherent existence a forest is perceived to be endowed with. That which is composed is inevitably empty. A forest is composed of trees and therefore empty. All compositions are empty. All compositions are devoid of inherent existence. To understand that a forest can as a composition not be endowed with inherent existence is to understand conceptually the emptiness of a forest.

## Mountain

A mountain is empty. A mountain is a composition of enormous rocks. That which is composed of rocks is dependent on rocks. That which is dependent on rocks cannot exist independently from rocks. That which cannot exist independently from rocks cannot exist independently from everything else. That which cannot exist independently from everything else cannot be endowed with inherent existence. That which cannot be endowed with inherent existence is devoid of inherent existence. That which is devoid of inherent existence is empty. A mountain is devoid of inherent existence. A mountain is empty. The emptiness of a mountain is the absence of inherent existence a mountain is perceived to be endowed with. That which is composed is inevitably empty. A mountain is composed of rocks and therefore empty. All compositions are empty. All compositions are devoid of inherent existence. To understand that a mountain can as a composition not be

14

endowed with inherent existence is to understand conceptually the emptiness of a mountain.

### River

A river is empty. A river is a composition of masses of water. That which is composed of masses of water is dependent on masses of water. That which is dependent on masses of water cannot exist independently from masses of water. That which cannot exist independently from masses of water cannot exist independently from everything else. That which cannot exist independently from everything else cannot be endowed with inherent existence. That which cannot be endowed with inherent existence is devoid of inherent existence. That which is devoid of inherent existence is empty. A river is devoid of inherent existence. A river is empty. The emptiness of a river is the absence of inherent existence a river is perceived to be endowed with. That which is composed is inevitably empty. A river is composed of masses of water and therefore empty. All compositions are empty. All compositions are devoid of inherent existence. To understand that a river can as a composition not be endowed with inherent existence is to understand conceptually the emptiness of a river.

### Contemplation

The emptiness of compositions can be understood conceptually. To contemplate and reflect on the emptiness of compositions is to cultivate a conceptual understanding of emptiness. Contemplation is the cause. Understanding is the effect. To contemplate the emptiness of compositions is to contemplate it a thousand times, ten thousand times, and a hundred thousand times.

# The fundamental absence of entities

### The fundamental absence of entities

Entities have never come into existence. Entities are fundamentally absent. That which is fundamentally absent is not. Entities are not. Entities are not entities. That which is fundamentally absent is inexpressible. Entities are inexpressible.

### The true nature of all

All is devoid of entities. Entities are fundamentally absent. The fundamental absence of entities is the true nature of all.

### The fundamental absence of entities

Entities are empty. Entities are devoid of inherent existence. The emptiness of entities is the absence of inherent existence entities are perceived to be endowed with. From the emptiness of entities follows the fundamental absence of entities. Entities are fundamentally absent.

### The fundamental absence of entities

An entity is an entity endowed with inherent existence. An entity and the inherent existence indwelling in an entity are inseparable. The absence of inherent existence indwelling in an entity is inevitably the absence of an entity. From the absence of inherent existence indwelling in an entity follows the absence of an entity. From the emptiness of an entity follows the fundamental absence of an entity.

### Water in a vessel

An entity and the inherent existence indwelling in an entity are inseparable. An entity and the inherent existence indwelling in an entity are like water in a vessel. Inherent existence is like a mass of water in a vessel. An entity is like the shape adopted by the water in the vessel but not the vessel itself.

The presence of water in a vessel is inevitably the presence of a shape adopted by water. A shape, however, cannot be adopted in the absence of water. The absence of water is inevitably the absence of a shape adopted by water. From the absence of water in a vessel follows the absence of a shape adopted by water.

Likewise, the presence of inherent existence indwelling in an entity is inevitably the presence of an entity. An entity, however, cannot be present in the absence of inherent existence. The absence of inherent existence is inevitably the absence of an entity. From the absence of inherent existence follows the absence of an entity.

The absence of inherent existence is like the absence of water in a vessel. The absence of an entity is like the absence of a shape adopted by water. From the absence of water in a vessel follows the absence of a shape adopted by water. From the absence of inherent existence indwelling in an entity follows the absence of an entity.

The absence of inherent existence indwelling in an entity is the emptiness of an entity. From the emptiness of an entity follows the fundamental absence of an entity.


### Entities are not entities

An entity is an entity endowed with inherent existence. An entity endowed with inherent existence is an entity.

An entity devoid of inherent existence is not an entity. An entity devoid of inherent existence is not.

# The fundamental absence of compositions

## The fundamental absence of compositions

Compositions are fundamentally absent. Compositions have never come into existence. A composition is an entity composed of smaller entities. A composition is a composition of smaller entities. Smaller entities cannot constitute a composition. Smaller entities cannot constitute a composition of smaller entities. A smaller entity can only constitute a smaller entity. A smaller entity can only constitute itself. A smaller entity and another smaller entity and yet other smaller entities do not come together and declare to constitute an entity. They do not come together and declare to constitute a composition of smaller entities. A composition of smaller entities has never come into existence. A composition of smaller entities is fundamentally absent. A composition is not a composition, because it is a composition. A composition is a composition and therefore not a composition. To understand conceptually the fundamental absence of compositions is to understand conceptually the emptiness of compositions. To understand one is to understand the other. To understand one is to understand both.

## Forest

A forest is fundamentally absent. A forest is an entity composed of trees. A forest is a composition of trees. Trees cannot constitute a forest. Trees cannot constitute a composition. A tree can only constitute a tree. A tree can only constitute itself. A tree and another tree and yet other trees do not come together and declare to constitute a forest. They do not come together and declare to constitute an entity. A forest has never come into existence. A forest is fundamentally absent. Compositions have never come into existence. Compositions are fundamentally absent. A forest is not a forest, because it is a composition. A forest is a composition and therefore not a forest. To understand conceptually the fundamental absence of a forest is to understand conceptually the emptiness of a forest. To understand one is to understand the other. To understand one is to understand both.

## Mountain

A mountain is fundamentally absent. A mountain is an entity composed of enormous rocks. A mountain is a composition of rocks. Rocks cannot constitute a mountain. Rocks cannot constitute a composition. A rock can only constitute a rock. A rock can only constitute itself. A rock and another rock and yet other rocks do not come together and declare to constitute a mountain. They do not come together and declare to constitute an entity. A mountain has never come into existence. A mountain is fundamentally absent. Compositions have never come into existence. Compositions are fundamentally absent. A mountain is not a mountain, because it is a composition. A mountain is a composition and therefore not a mountain. To understand conceptually the fundamental absence of a mountain is to understand conceptually the emptiness of a mountain.

A rock is fundamentally absent. A rock is an entity composed of smaller rocks. A rock is a composition of smaller rocks. To break apart a rock is to reveal the presence of smaller rocks. Smaller rocks cannot constitute a rock. Smaller rocks cannot constitute a composition. A smaller rock can only constitute a smaller rock. A smaller rock can only constitute itself. A smaller rock and another smaller rock and yet other smaller rocks do not come together and declare to constitute a rock. They do not come together and declare to constitute an entity. A rock has never come into existence. A rock is fundamentally absent. Compositions have never come into existence. Compositions are fundamentally absent. A rock is not a rock, because it is a composition. A rock is a composition and therefore not a rock. A mountain is fundamentally absent and so are the rocks that constitute a mountain.

**River**

A river is fundamentally absent. A river is an entity composed of masses of water. A river is a composition of masses of water. Masses of water cannot constitute a river. Masses of water cannot constitute a composition. A mass of water can only constitute a mass of water. A mass of water can only constitute itself. A mass of water and another mass of water and yet other masses of water do not come together and declare to constitute a river. They do not come together and declare to constitute an entity. A river has never come into existence. A river is fundamentally absent. Compositions have never come into existence. Compositions are fundamentally absent. A river is not a river, because it is a composition. A river is a composition and therefore not a river. To understand conceptually the fundamental absence of a river is to understand conceptually the emptiness of a river. To understand conceptually the fundamental absence of a river is to understand conceptually the fundamental absence of a lake, a sea, and an ocean.

**Contemplation**

The fundamental absence of compositions can be understood conceptually. To contemplate and reflect on the fundamental absence of compositions is to cultivate a conceptual understanding of the fundamental absence of entities. Contemplation is the cause. Understanding is the effect. To contemplate the fundamental absence of compositions is to contemplate it a thousand times, ten thousand times, and a hundred thousand times.

# Dust particles

## The emptiness of a composition of dust particles

A composition of dust particles is empty. A composition of dust particles is devoid of inherent existence. A dust particle is the smallest perceptible entity. The smallest perceptible entity is called a dust particle. That which is composed of dust particles is dependent on dust particles. That which is dependent on dust particles cannot exist independently from dust particles. That which cannot exist independently from dust particles cannot exist independently from everything else. That which cannot exist independently from everything else cannot be endowed with inherent existence. That which cannot be endowed with inherent existence is devoid of inherent existence. That which is devoid of inherent existence is empty. A composition of dust particles is devoid of inherent existence. A composition of dust particles is empty. The emptiness of a composition of dust particles is the absence of inherent existence a composition of dust particles is perceived to be endowed with. That which is composed is inevitably empty. A composition of dust particles is empty. To understand that a composition of dust particles cannot be endowed with inherent existence is to understand the impossibility of a composition of dust particles to be endowed with inherent existence. To understand that a composition of dust particles cannot be endowed with inherent existence is to understand conceptually the emptiness of a composition of dust particles.

**The fundamental absence of a composition of dust particles**

A composition of dust particles is fundamentally absent. A dust particle is the smallest perceptible entity. The smallest perceptible entity is called a dust particle. Dust particles cannot constitute an entity. Dust particles cannot constitute a composition of dust particles. A dust particle can only constitute a dust particle. A dust particle can only constitute itself. A dust particle and another dust particle and yet other masses of dust particles do not come together and declare to constitute an entity. They do not come together and declare to constitute a composition of dust particles. A composition of dust particles has never come into existence. A composition of dust particles is fundamentally absent. A composition of dust particles is not a composition of dust particles, because it is a composition of dust particles. A composition of dust particles is a composition of dust particles and therefore not a composition of dust particles. To understand conceptually the fundamental absence of a composition of dust particles is to understand conceptually the emptiness of a composition of dust particles.


**The emptiness of the smallest entity**

Compositions are empty. Compositions are devoid of inherent existence. The smallest entity is not a composition. The smallest entity cannot be composed of smaller entities, because it is the smallest entity. The smallest entity is empty, even though it is not a composition. The smallest entity is devoid of inherent existence, even though it is not a composition. The emptiness of entities is a quality of entities. The absence of inherent existence is a quality of entities. The emptiness of entities inheres in all entities. It inheres in entities that are composed as well as in entities that are not composed. That which is composed is devoid of inherent existence. That which is not composed is devoid of inherent existence. All is devoid of inherent existence.

# Form

### The emptiness of form

The Buddha teaches that all is empty. Form is empty. Form is the first skandha. The five skandhas are form, feeling, thinking, volition, and consciousness. The emptiness of form is the absence of inherent existence form is perceived to be endowed with. The emptiness of form can be contemplated by contemplating the emptiness of compositions. Form is matter. Entities pertaining to matter are composed of smaller entities. Entities pertaining to matter are compositions. Compositions are empty. Compositions are devoid of inherent existence. Entities pertaining to form are empty. Entities pertaining to form are devoid of inherent existence. To understand the emptiness of compositions is to understand the emptiness of entities that pertain to and arise from form. To understand the emptiness of compositions is to understand the emptiness of form.

### The fundamental absence of form

Form is fundamentally absent. Form is the first skandha. The fundamental absence of form can be contemplated by contemplating the fundamental absence of compositions. Form is matter. Entities pertaining to matter are composed of smaller entities. Entities pertaining to matter are compositions. Compositions are fundamentally absent. Compositions have never come into existence. Entities pertaining to form are fundamentally absent. Entities pertaining to form have never come into existence. To understand the fundamental absence of compositions is to understand the fundamental absence of entities that pertain to and arise from form. To understand the fundamental absence of compositions is to understand the fundamental absence of form.

# The true nature of all

### Empty and fundamentally absent

Entities are empty and fundamentally absent. The emptiness and fundamental absence of entities are the absence of entities endowed with inherent existence. The emptiness and fundamental absence of entities are the absence of inherently existent entities.

### The emptiness of entities

The emptiness of entities is the true nature of all. All is devoid of inherent existence. Inherent existence is fundamentally absent.

### The fundamental absence of entities

The fundamental absence of entities is the true nature of all. All is devoid of entities. Entities are fundamentally absent.

### The true nature of all

The emptiness and fundamental absence of entities are the true nature of all. All is devoid of inherently existent entities. Inherently existent entities are fundamentally absent.

### The true nature of all

The true nature of all is the absence of inherently existent entities. The absence of inherently existent entities is the true nature of all.

### Perception

The true nature of all is revealed in the absence of the perception of inherently existent entities. The absence of the perception of inherently existent entities reveals the true nature of all.

# All is mind

### The notion of an entity

The mind perceives the presence of entities. The perception of an entity is caused by the presence of the notion of an entity. The notion of an entity arises from the mind. It comes into being by way of thinking. Thinking is the coming together of the mind, the notion of an entity, and the consciousness of the mind. The mind constitutes the sixth sense. The notion of an entity pertains to the sixth sense object. The consciousness of the mind constitutes the sixth sense consciousness. The mind fabricates the notion of an entity and it mistakes the presence of the notion of an entity for a truly existent entity. The perception of an entity arises entirely from the mind. An entity perceived by the mind is the notion of an entity fabricated by the mind.

### The notion of inherent existence

The mind perceives the presence of entities. Entities perceived by the mind are perceived to be endowed with inherent existence. To perceive an entity to be endowed with inherent existence is to perceive an entity to exist independently from everything else. To perceive an entity to be endowed with inherent existence is to perceive an entity to exist by itself and in itself. The perception of inherent existence is caused by the presence of the notion of inherent existence. The notion of inherent existence arises from the mind. It comes into being by way of thinking. Thinking is the coming together of the mind, the notion of inherent existence, and the consciousness of the mind. The mind gives rise to the notion of inherent existence and it mistakes the presence of the notion of inherent existence for inherent existence. The perception of inherent existence arises entirely from the mind. Inherent existence perceived by the mind is the notion of inherent existence fabricated by the mind.

### Forest

The mind perceives the presence of entities. The mind perceives the presence of a forest. The perception of a forest is caused by the presence of the notion of a forest. The notion of a forest comes into being by way of thinking. Thinking is the coming together of the mind, the notion of a forest, and the consciousness of the mind. The mind fabricates the notion of a forest and it mistakes the presence of the notion of a forest for a truly existent forest.

A forest perceived by the mind is perceived to be endowed with inherent existence. The perception of inherent existence is caused by the presence of the notion of inherent existence. The notion of inherent existence comes into being by way of thinking. Thinking is the coming together of the mind, the notion of inherent existence, and the consciousness of the mind. The mind fabricates the notion of inherent existence and it falsely perceives a forest to be endowed with inherent existence.

A forest perceived by the mind is the notion of a forest fabricated by the mind. Inherent existence a forest is perceived to be endowed with is the notion of inherent existence fabricated by the mind.

### Mountain

The mind perceives the presence of entities. The mind perceives the presence of a mountain. The perception of a mountain is caused by the presence of the notion of a mountain. The notion of a mountain comes into being by way of thinking. Thinking is the coming together of the mind, the notion of a mountain, and the consciousness of the mind. The mind fabricates the notion of a mountain and it mistakes the presence of the notion of a mountain for a truly existent mountain.

A mountain perceived by the mind is perceived to be endowed with inherent existence. The perception of inherent existence is caused by the presence of the notion of inherent existence. The notion of inherent existence comes into being by way of thinking. Thinking is the coming together of the mind, the notion of inherent existence, and the consciousness of the mind. The mind fabricates the notion of inherent existence and it falsely perceives a mountain to be endowed with inherent existence.

A mountain perceived by the mind is the notion of a mountain fabricated by the mind. Inherent existence a mountain is perceived to be endowed with is the notion of inherent existence fabricated by the mind.


### River

The mind perceives the presence of entities. The mind perceives the presence of a river. The perception of a river is caused by the presence of the notion of a river. The notion of a river comes into being by way of thinking. Thinking is the coming together of the mind, the notion of a river, and the consciousness of the mind. The mind fabricates the notion of a river and it mistakes the presence of the notion of a river for a truly existent river.

A river perceived by the mind is perceived to be endowed with inherent existence. The perception of inherent existence is caused by the presence of the notion of inherent existence. The notion of inherent existence comes into being by way of thinking. Thinking is the coming together of the mind, the notion of inherent existence, and the consciousness of the mind. The mind fabricates the notion of inherent existence and it falsely perceives a river to be endowed with inherent existence.

A river perceived by the mind is the notion of a river fabricated by the mind. Inherent existence a river is perceived to be endowed with is the notion of inherent existence fabricated by the mind.

# Perception

### The perception of entities

The mind perceives the presence of entities. Entities, however, have never come into existence. Entities are fundamentally absent. The mind perceives that which has never come into existence. The mind perceives that which is fundamentally absent. An entity perceived by the mind is the notion of an entity fabricated by the mind. The mind gives rise to the notion of an entity and it mistakes the presence of the notion of an entity for a truly existent entity. The presence of the notion of an entity causes the perception of an entity. The presence of the notion of an entity causes the perception of that which is fundamentally absent. The mind perceives that which is fundamentally absent, because it fabricates a notion of that which is fundamentally absent. The perception of entities is a fundamental flaw of the mind.

### The perception of inherent existence

The mind perceives inherent existence. Inherent existence, however, is fundamentally absent. All is devoid of inherent existence. The mind perceives the absence of inherent existence to be endowed with inherent existence. The perception of inherent existence is caused by the presence of the notion of inherent existence. The mind gives rise to the notion of inherent existence and it mistakes the presence of the notion of inherent existence for inherent existence. The presence of the notion of inherent existence causes the perception of inherent existence. The presence of the notion of inherent existence causes the perception of that which is fundamentally absent. The mind perceives the absence of inherent existence to be endowed with inherent existence, because it fabricates the notion of inherent existence. The perception of inherent existence is a fundamental flaw of the mind.

## Illusion

The Diamond Sutra says, "All perceptions are illusory." The word 'perception' refers to the perception of entities. The word 'perception' also refers to the perception of inherent existence. The perception of entities is illusory. The perception of inherent existence is illusory. All perceptions are illusory.

## Forest

The mind perceives the presence of entities. The mind perceives the presence of a forest. A forest, however, has never come into existence. A forest is fundamentally absent. The perception of a forest is caused by the presence of the notion of a forest. A forest perceived by the mind is the notion of a forest fabricated by the mind. The mind perceives that which is fundamentally absent, because it fabricates a notion of that which is fundamentally absent.

The mind perceives a forest to be endowed with inherent existence. A forest, however, is devoid of inherent existence. All is devoid of inherent existence. Inherent existence is fundamentally absent. The perception of inherent existence is caused by the presence of the notion of inherent existence. The mind perceives that which is devoid of inherent existence to be endowed with inherent existence, because it fabricates the notion of inherent existence.

## Mountain

The mind perceives the presence of entities. The mind perceives the presence of a mountain. A mountain, however, has never come into existence. A mountain is fundamentally absent. The perception of a mountain is caused by the presence of the notion of a mountain. A mountain perceived by the mind is the notion of a mountain fabricated by the mind. The mind perceives that which is fundamentally absent, because it fabricates a notion of that which is fundamentally absent.

The mind perceives a mountain to be endowed with inherent existence. A mountain, however, is devoid of inherent existence. All is devoid of inherent existence. Inherent existence is fundamentally absent. The perception of inherent existence is caused by the presence of the notion of inherent existence. The mind perceives that which is devoid of inherent existence to be endowed with inherent existence, because it fabricates the notion of inherent existence.

### River

The mind perceives the presence of entities. The mind perceives the presence of a river. A river, however, has never come into existence. A river is fundamentally absent. The perception of a river is caused by the presence of the notion of a river. A river perceived by the mind is the notion of a river fabricated by the mind. The mind perceives that which is fundamentally absent, because it fabricates a notion of that which is fundamentally absent.

The mind perceives a river to be endowed with inherent existence. A river, however, is devoid of inherent existence. All is devoid of inherent existence. Inherent existence is fundamentally absent. The perception of inherent existence is caused by the presence of the notion of inherent existence. The mind perceives that which is devoid of inherent existence to be endowed with inherent existence, because it fabricates the notion of inherent existence.

# Inherently existent entities

### Inherently existent entities

The mind perceives inherently existent entities. An inherently existent entity is an entity endowed with inherent existence. The perception of an inherently existent entity is caused by the presence of the notion of an entity and the presence of the notion of inherent existence. The notion of an entity and the notion of inherent existence come into being by way of thinking. Thinking is the coming together of the mind, notions, and the consciousness of the mind. The mind gives rise to the notion of an entity and the notion of inherent existence and it mistakes the presence of the notion of an entity and the presence of the notion of inherent existence for an inherently existent entity. An entity perceived by the mind is the notion of an entity fabricated by the mind. Inherent existence an entity is perceived to be endowed with is the notion of inherent existence fabricated by the mind. The perception of an inherently existent entity arises entirely from the mind.

### Forest

The mind perceives the presence of a forest. A forest perceived by the mind is perceived to be endowed with inherent existence. A forest is an inherently existent forest. The perception of an inherently existent forest is caused by the presence of the notion of a forest and the presence of the notion of inherent existence. The mind gives rise to the notion of a forest and the notion of inherent existence and it mistakes the presence of the notion of a forest and the presence of the notion of inherent existence for an inherently existent forest. The perception of an inherently existent forest arises entirely from the mind.

## Mountain

The mind perceives the presence of a mountain. A mountain perceived by the mind is perceived to be endowed with inherent existence. A mountain is an inherently existent mountain. The perception of an inherently existent mountain is caused by the presence of the notion of a mountain and the presence of the notion of inherent existence. The mind gives rise to the notion of a mountain and the notion of inherent existence and it mistakes the presence of the notion of a mountain and the presence of the notion of inherent existence for an inherently existent mountain. The perception of an inherently existent mountain arises entirely from the mind.

## River

The mind perceives the presence of a river. A river perceived by the mind is perceived to be endowed with inherent existence. A river is an inherently existent river. The perception of an inherently existent river is caused by the presence of the notion of a river and the presence of the notion of inherent existence. The mind gives rise to the notion of a river and the notion of inherent existence and it mistakes the presence of the notion of a river and the presence of the notion of inherent existence for an inherently existent river. The perception of an inherently existent river arises entirely from the mind.

# The emptiness of a world

### A world

The mind perceives the presence of entities. The mind perceives the presence of a world. A world is an entity. A world perceived by the mind is perceived to be endowed with inherent existence. To perceive a world to be endowed with inherent existence is to perceive a world to exist independently from everything else. To perceive a world to be endowed with inherent existence is to perceive a world as a separate and distinct entity. A world is a world endowed with inherent existence. A world is an inherently existent world. A world and the inherent existence indwelling in a world are inseparable.

### The emptiness of a world

A world is empty. A world is devoid of inherent existence. The emptiness of a world is the absence of inherent existence a world is perceived to be endowed with. The emptiness of a world is the true nature of a world. The absence of inherent existence is the true nature of a world.

### The emptiness of a world

A world is empty. A world is devoid of inherent existence. A world is a mass of dust particles. A mass of dust particles is a composition of dust particles. A dust particle is the smallest perceptible entity. The smallest perceptible entity is called a dust particle. That which is composed of dust particles is dependent on dust particles. That which is dependent on dust particles cannot exist independently from dust particles. That which cannot exist independently from dust particles cannot exist independently from everything else. That which cannot exist independently from everything else cannot be endowed with inherent existence. That which cannot be endowed with inherent existence is devoid of inherent

33

existence. That which is devoid of inherent existence is empty. A mass of dust particles is devoid of inherent existence. A mass of dust particles is empty. A world is devoid of inherent existence. A world is empty. The emptiness of a mass of dust particles is the absence of inherent existence a mass of dust particles is perceived to be endowed with. The emptiness of a world is the absence of inherent existence a world is perceived to be endowed with. That which is composed is inevitably empty. A world is composed of dust particles and therefore empty.

### The fundamental absence of a world

A world is fundamentally absent. A world has never come into existence. That which is fundamentally absent is not. A world is not. A world is not a world. That which is fundamentally absent is inexpressible. A world is inexpressible. The fundamental absence of a world is the true nature of a world.

### The fundamental absence of a world

A world is empty. A world is devoid of inherent existence. The emptiness of a world is the absence of inherent existence a world is perceived to be endowed with. From the absence of inherent existence indwelling in a world follows the absence of a world. From the emptiness of a world follows the fundamental absence of a world. A world devoid of inherent existence is not a world. A world devoid of inherent existence is not. A world is fundamentally absent.

## The fundamental absence of a world

A world is fundamentally absent. A world is a mass of dust particles. A mass of dust particles is a composition of dust particles. Dust particles cannot constitute a world. Dust particles cannot constitute a mass of dust particles. A dust particle can only constitute a dust particle. A dust particle can only constitute itself. A dust particle and another dust particle and yet other myriads of dust particles do not come together and declare to constitute a world. They do not come together and declare to constitute an entity. A world has never come into existence. A world is fundamentally absent. A mass of dust particles has never come into existence. A mass of dust particles is fundamentally absent. A mass of dust particles is not a mass of dust particles, because it is a mass of dust particles. A mass of dust particles is a mass of dust particles and therefore not a mass of dust particles. A world is not a world, because it is a composition. A world is a composition and therefore not a world.

## The notion of a world

The mind perceives the presence of a world. The perception of a world is caused by the presence of the notion of a world. The notion of a world arises from the mind. The mind is that which gives rise to the notion of a world. The notion of a world comes into being by way of thinking. Thinking is the coming together of the mind, the notion of a world, and the consciousness of the mind. The mind fabricates the notion of a world and it mistakes the presence of the notion of a world for a truly existent world. A world perceived by the mind is the notion of a world fabricated by the mind. The notion of a world is merely a name. A world perceived by the mind is merely a name.

### The notion of inherent existence

The mind perceives the presence of a world. A world perceived by the mind is perceived to be endowed with inherent existence. The perception of inherent existence is caused by the presence of the notion of inherent existence. The notion of inherent existence arises from the mind. The mind is that which gives rise to the notion of inherent existence. The mind fabricates the notion of inherent existence and it mistakes the presence of the notion of inherent existence for inherent existence. Inherent existence a world is perceived to be endowed with is the notion of inherent existence fabricated by the mind.

### An inherently existent world

The mind perceives the presence of an inherently existent world. An inherently existent world is a world endowed with inherent existence. The perception of an inherently existent world is caused by the presence of the notion of a world and the presence of the notion of inherent existence. The mind gives rise to the notion of a world and the notion of inherent existence and it mistakes the presence of the notion of a world and the presence of the notion of inherent existence for an inherently existent world.

### Perception

The mind perceives the presence of a world. A world, however, has never come into existence. A world is fundamentally absent. The perception of a world is caused by the presence of the notion of a world. A world perceived by the mind is the notion of a world fabricated by the mind. The mind perceives that which is fundamentally absent, because it fabricates a notion of that which is fundamentally absent.

The mind perceives a world to be endowed with inherent existence. A world, however, is devoid of inherent existence. All is devoid of inherent existence. The perception of inherent existence is caused by the presence of the notion of inherent existence. The mind perceives that which

36

is devoid of inherent existence to be endowed with inherent existence, because it fabricates the notion of inherent existence.

### A mass of dust particles

The Diamond Sutra says, " 'Subhuti, what do you think? If good men and good women broke apart and ground a three thousand great thousand world into dust particles, would there not be many dust particles?' Subhuti said, 'There would be indeed many, World Honored One. Why? If a mass of dust particles was endowed with existence, the Buddha would not call it a mass of dust particles. Why? The Buddha says that a mass of dust particles is not a mass of dust particles. It is named a mass of dust particles. World Honored One, a three thousand great thousand world, the Tathagata speaks of, is not a world. It is named a world. Why? If a world was endowed with existence, it would be a composition. The Tathagata says that a composition is not a composition. It is named a composition.' 'Subhuti, compositions are inexpressible, but the common people are attached to such things.' "

The Diamond Sutra is the Sutra of the Perfection of Diamond Wisdom. The Diamond Sutra is a discourse of the Buddha on the bodhisattva way, the perfection of wisdom, and unsurpassed complete enlightenment. "World Honored One" and "Tathagata" are epithets of the Buddha. The epithet 'World Honored One' is derived from the Sanskrit word 'Bhagavan'. The epithet 'Tathagata' is Sanskrit and means 'Thus Come One'. Subhuti is the interlocutor of the Diamond Sutra. He was one of the ten major disciples of the Buddha.

A three thousand great thousand world is a world system composed of one billion worlds. A three thousand great thousand world is also composed of a mass of dust particles. To break apart and grind such a world system into dust particles is to reveal the presence of a mass of dust particles. A mass of dust particles is a composition of dust particles. A three thousand great thousand world is empty, because it is a composition of dust particles. A three thousand great thousand world is fundamentally absent, because it is a composition of dust particles.

# Two notions

### Thinking

The mind constitutes the sixth sense. Notions constitute the sixth sense object. The consciousness of the mind constitutes the sixth sense consciousness. Thinking is the coming together of the mind, notions, and the consciousness of the mind.

An entity perceived by the mind is the notion of an entity fabricated by the mind. The notion of an entity comes into being by way of thinking. Thinking is the coming together of the mind, the notion of an entity, and the consciousness of the mind.

Inherent existence perceived by the mind is the notion of inherent existence fabricated by the mind. The notion of inherent existence comes into being by way of thinking. Thinking is the coming together of the mind, the notion of inherent existence, and the consciousness of the mind.

### Formation and cessation

The formation of the notion of an entity is the beginning of the notion of an entity. The cessation of the notion of an entity is the end of the notion of an entity. The notion of an entity is present between its formation and cessation. The presence of the notion of an entity causes the perception of a truly existent entity.

The formation of the notion of inherent existence is the beginning of the notion of inherent existence. The cessation of the notion of inherent existence is the end of the notion of inherent existence. The notion of inherent existence is present between its formation and cessation. The presence of the notion of inherent existence causes the perception of inherent existence.

## Two notions

The notion of an entity comes into being in the presence of the notion of inherent existence. The arising of the notion of an entity is dependent on the presence of the notion of inherent existence. The presence of the notion of an entity is the presence of the notion of an entity and the presence of the notion of inherent existence.

## Habit of mind

Entities perceived by the mind are notions of entities fabricated by the mind. The mind has been fabricating notions of entities since time without beginning. The formation of notions of entities has become an incessant habit of mind.

Inherent existence perceived by the mind is the notion of inherent existence fabricated by the mind. The mind has been fabricating the notion of inherent existence since time without beginning. The formation of the notion of inherent existence has become an incessant habit of mind.

## Quickness

Notions of entities arise fast. The time needed for the mind to form and complete the notion of an entity is short. The mind is fast at fabricating notions of entities. It has been fabricating notions of entities since time without beginning. The quickness of the arising of the notion of an entity stems from the mind's habit of fabricating the notion of an entity.

The notion of inherent existence arises fast. The time needed for the mind to form and complete the notion of inherent existence is short. The mind is fast at fabricating the notion of inherent existence. It has been fabricating the notion of inherent existence since time without beginning. The quickness of the arising of the notion of inherent existence stems from the mind's habit of fabricating the notion of inherent existence.

### Fierceness

Entities perceived by the mind are notions of entities fabricated by the mind. The mind has been fabricating notions of entities since time without beginning. The formation of notions of entities has become an incessant habit of mind. Notions of entities arise fast. Notions of entities arise fiercely. The fierceness of the arising of the notion of an entity is the mind's compulsion to fabricate the notion of an entity.

Inherent existence perceived by the mind is the notion of inherent existence fabricated by the mind. The mind has been fabricating the notion of inherent existence since time without beginning. The formation of the notion of inherent existence has become an incessant habit of mind. The notion of inherent existence arises fast. The notion of inherent existence arises fiercely. The fierceness of the arising of the notion of inherent existence is the mind's compulsion to fabricate the notion of inherent existence.


### A continuation of notions

The notion of an entity forms and ceases from moment to moment. A notion of an entity that was is followed by a notion of an entity that is. A notion of an entity that is is followed by a notion of an entity that will be. The notion of an entity is a succession of notions. The notion of an entity is a continuation of notions. An entity perceived by the mind is the notion of an entity fabricated by the mind. An entity perceived by the mind is a continuation of notions fabricated by the mind.

The notion of inherent existence forms and ceases from moment to moment. A notion of inherent existence that was is followed by a notion of inherent existence that is. A notion of inherent existence that is is followed by a notion of inherent existence that will be. The notion of inherent existence is a succession of notions. The notion of inherent existence is a continuation of notions. Inherent existence perceived by the mind is the notion of inherent existence fabricated by the mind. Inherent existence perceived by the mind is a continuation of notions fabricated by the mind.

### Constant presence

The mind is constantly fabricating notions of entities. The constant formation of notions of entities is the constant presence of notions of entities. The constant presence of notions of entities is the constant perception of truly existent entities.

The mind is constantly fabricating the notion of inherent existence. The constant formation of the notion of inherent existence is the constant presence of the notion of inherent existence. The constant presence of the notion of inherent existence is the constant perception of inherent existence.

# Revealing the true nature of all

### The fundamental absence of entities

Entities are fundamentally absent. Entities have never come into existence. The fundamental absence of an entity is revealed in the absence of the notion of an entity. The perception of an entity is caused by the presence of the notion of an entity. The perception of an entity does not come into being in the absence of the notion of an entity. The absence of the notion of an entity is the absence of the perception of an entity. The absence of the perception of an entity reveals the fundamental absence of an entity. The fundamental absence of an entity is revealed in the absence of the notion of an entity.

### The emptiness of entities

Entities are empty. Entities are devoid of inherent existence. The emptiness of an entity is the absence of inherent existence an entity is perceived to be endowed with. The emptiness of an entity is revealed in the absence of the notion of inherent existence. The perception of inherent existence is caused by the presence of the notion of inherent existence. The perception of inherent existence does not come into being in the absence of the notion of inherent existence. The absence of the notion of inherent existence is the absence of the perception of inherent existence. The absence of the perception of inherent existence reveals the emptiness of an entity. The emptiness of an entity is revealed in the absence of the notion of inherent existence.

## Forest

A forest is fundamentally absent. A forest has never come into existence. The fundamental absence of a forest is revealed in the absence of the notion of a forest. The perception of a forest is caused by the presence of the notion of a forest. The perception of a forest does not come into being in the absence of the notion of a forest. The absence of the notion of a forest is the absence of the perception of a forest. The absence of the perception of a forest reveals the fundamental absence of a forest. The fundamental absence of a forest is revealed in the absence of the notion of a forest.

A forest is empty. A forest is devoid of inherent existence. The emptiness of a forest is the absence of inherent existence a forest is perceived to be endowed with. The emptiness of a forest is revealed in the absence of the notion of inherent existence. The perception of inherent existence is caused by the presence of the notion of inherent existence. The perception of inherent existence does not come into being in the absence of the notion of inherent existence. The absence of the notion of inherent existence is the absence of the perception of inherent existence. The absence of the perception of inherent existence reveals the emptiness of a forest. The emptiness of a forest is revealed in the absence of the notion of inherent existence.


## Mountain

A mountain is fundamentally absent. A mountain has never come into existence. The fundamental absence of a mountain is revealed in the absence of the notion of a mountain. The perception of a mountain is caused by the presence of the notion of a mountain. The perception of a mountain does not come into being in the absence of the notion of a mountain. The absence of the notion of a mountain is the absence of the perception of a mountain. The absence of the perception of a mountain reveals the fundamental absence of a mountain. The fundamental absence of a mountain is revealed in the absence of the notion of a mountain.

A mountain is empty. A mountain is devoid of inherent existence. The emptiness of a mountain is the absence of inherent existence a mountain is perceived to be endowed with. The emptiness of a mountain is revealed in the absence of the notion of inherent existence. The perception of inherent existence is caused by the presence of the notion of inherent existence. The perception of inherent existence does not come into being in the absence of the notion of inherent existence. The absence of the notion of inherent existence is the absence of the perception of inherent existence. The absence of the perception of inherent existence reveals the emptiness of a mountain. The emptiness of a mountain is revealed in the absence of the notion of inherent existence.

### River

A river is fundamentally absent. A river has never come into existence. The fundamental absence of a river is revealed in the absence of the notion of a river. The perception of a river is caused by the presence of the notion of a river. The perception of a river does not come into being in the absence of the notion of a river. The absence of the notion of a river is the absence of the perception of a river. The absence of the perception of a river reveals the fundamental absence of a river. The fundamental absence of a river is revealed in the absence of the notion of a river.

A river is empty. A river is devoid of inherent existence. The emptiness of a river is the absence of inherent existence a river is perceived to be endowed with. The emptiness of a river is revealed in the absence of the notion of inherent existence. The perception of inherent existence is caused by the presence of the notion of inherent existence. The perception of inherent existence does not come into being in the absence of the notion of inherent existence. The absence of the notion of inherent existence is the absence of the perception of inherent existence. The absence of the perception of inherent existence reveals the emptiness of a river. The emptiness of a river is revealed in the absence of the notion of inherent existence.

# Revealing the true nature of all

## The emptiness and fundamental absence of entities

Entities are empty and fundamentally absent. The emptiness and fundamental absence of an entity are revealed in the absence of the notion of an entity and the absence of the notion of inherent existence. The perception of an inherently existent entity is caused by the presence of the notion of an entity and the presence of the notion of inherent existence. The perception of an inherently existent entity does not come into being in the absence of the notion of an entity and the absence of the notion of inherent existence. The absence of the notion of an entity and the absence of the notion of inherent existence are the absence of an entity perceived to exist inherently and the absence of inherent existence an entity is perceived to be endowed with. The absence of inherent existence an entity is perceived to be endowed with is the emptiness of an entity. The emptiness and fundamental absence of an entity are revealed in the absence of the notion of an entity and the absence of the notion of inherent existence.

## The true nature of all

The emptiness and fundamental absence of entities are the true nature of all. The emptiness and fundamental absence of entities are revealed in the absence of the notion of inherent existence and the absence of all notions of entities. The true nature of all is revealed in the absence of the notion of inherent existence and the absence of all notions of entities.

### Forest

A forest is empty and fundamentally absent. The emptiness and fundamental absence of a forest are revealed in the absence of the notion of a forest and the absence of the notion of inherent existence. The perception of an inherently existent forest is caused by the presence of the notion of a forest and the presence of the notion of inherent existence. The perception of an inherently existent forest does not come into being in the absence of the notion of a forest and the absence of the notion of inherent existence. The absence of the notion of a forest and the absence of the notion of inherent existence are the absence of a forest perceived to exist inherently and the absence of inherent existence a forest is perceived to be endowed with. The absence of inherent existence a forest is perceived to be endowed with is the emptiness of a forest. The emptiness and fundamental absence of a forest are revealed in the absence of the notion of a forest and the absence of the notion of inherent existence.

### Mountain

A mountain is empty and fundamentally absent. The emptiness and fundamental absence of a mountain are revealed in the absence of the notion of a mountain and the absence of the notion of inherent existence. The perception of an inherently existent mountain is caused by the presence of the notion of a mountain and the presence of the notion of inherent existence. The perception of an inherently existent mountain does not come into being in the absence of the notion of a mountain and the absence of the notion of inherent existence. The absence of the notion of a mountain and the absence of the notion of inherent existence are the absence of a mountain perceived to exist inherently and the absence of inherent existence a mountain is perceived to be endowed with. The absence of inherent existence a mountain is perceived to be endowed with is the emptiness of a mountain. The emptiness and fundamental absence of a mountain are revealed in the absence of the notion of a mountain and the absence of the notion of inherent existence.

## River

A river is empty and fundamentally absent. The emptiness and fundamental absence of a river are revealed in the absence of the notion of a river and the absence of the notion of inherent existence. The perception of an inherently existent river is caused by the presence of the notion of a river and the presence of the notion of inherent existence. The perception of an inherently existent river does not come into being in the absence of the notion of a river and the absence of the notion of inherent existence. The absence of the notion of a river and the absence of the notion of inherent existence are the absence of a river perceived to exist inherently and the absence of inherent existence a river is perceived to be endowed with. The absence of inherent existence a river is perceived to be endowed with is the emptiness of a river. The emptiness and fundamental absence of a river are revealed in the absence of the notion of a river and the absence of the notion of inherent existence.

# Detachment

### Revealing the true nature of all

All is empty and fundamentally absent. The emptiness and fundamental absence of entities are the true nature of all. The emptiness and fundamental absence of an entity are revealed in the absence of the notion of an entity and the absence of the notion of inherent existence. The absence of the notion of an entity and the absence of the notion of inherent existence can be arrived at by detaching from the notion of an entity. The absence of the notion of an entity and the absence of the notion of inherent existence can also be arrived at by detaching from the notion of inherent existence.

### Detachment from the notion of an entity

To detach from the notion of an entity is to not entertain the notion of an entity. To detach from the notion of an entity is to discontinue the formation of the notion of an entity. To detach from the notion of an entity is to seek the immediate absence of the notion of an entity. To detach from the notion of an entity is to withstand the fierceness of the arising of the notion of an entity. To detach from the notion of an entity is to endure patiently the absence of the notion of an entity.

### Detachment from the notion of inherent existence

To detach from the notion of inherent existence is to not entertain the notion of inherent existence. To detach from the notion of inherent existence is to discontinue the formation of the notion of inherent existence. To detach from the notion of inherent existence is to seek the immediate absence of the notion of inherent existence. To detach from the notion of inherent existence is to withstand the fierceness of the arising of the notion of inherent existence. To detach from the notion of inherent existence is to endure patiently the absence of the notion of inherent existence.

### Discontinue the formation

The formation of the notion of an entity is the beginning of the notion of an entity. The cessation of the notion of an entity is the end of the notion of an entity. The notion of an entity is present between its formation and cessation. The presence of the notion of an entity causes the perception of an entity. To detach from the notion of an entity is to arrive at the absence of the notion of an entity. To detach from the notion of an entity is to cease the presence of the notion of an entity. The presence of the notion of an entity is ceased by discontinuing the formation of the notion of an entity. To detach from the notion of an entity is to discontinue the formation of the notion of an entity.

### Discontinue the formation

The formation of the notion of inherent existence is the beginning of the notion of inherent existence. The cessation of the notion of inherent existence is the end of the notion of inherent existence. The notion of inherent existence is present between its formation and cessation. The presence of the notion of inherent existence causes the perception of inherent existence. To detach from the notion of inherent existence is to arrive at the absence of the notion of inherent existence. To detach from the notion of inherent existence is to cease the presence of the notion of inherent existence. The presence of the notion of inherent existence is ceased by discontinuing the formation of the notion of inherent existence. To detach from the notion of inherent existence is to discontinue the formation of the notion of inherent existence.

### Seek the immediate absence

Notions of entities arise fast. The time needed for the mind to form the notion of an entity is short. Even though the amount of time is short, the mind still requires time to form and complete the notion of an entity. Forming the notion of an entity is like an artist drawing a picture. Time is needed to draw and complete a picture. Time is needed to form and complete the notion of an entity. The mind is fast at fabricating the notion of an entity. The mind must be faster at detaching from the notion of an entity. To detach from the notion of an entity is to seek the immediate absence of the notion of an entity.

### Seek the immediate absence

The notion of inherent existence arises fast. The time needed for the mind to form the notion of inherent existence is short. Even though the amount of time is short, the mind still requires time to form and complete the notion of inherent existence. Forming the notion of inherent existence is like filling a vessel with water. Time is needed to fill a vessel with water. Time is needed to form and complete the notion of inherent existence. The mind is fast at fabricating the notion of inherent existence. The mind must be faster at detaching from the notion of inherent existence. To detach from the notion of inherent existence is to seek the immediate absence of the notion of inherent existence.

### Withstand the fierceness

Notions of entities arise fast. Notions of entities arise fiercely. The mind has been fabricating notions of entities since time without beginning. The fierceness of the arising of the notion of an entity is the mind's compulsion to fabricate the notion of an entity. To detach from the notion of an entity is to withstand the fierceness of the arising of the notion of an entity. To detach from the notion of an entity is to oppose the mind's compulsion to fabricate the notion of an entity.

## Withstand the fierceness

The notion of inherent existence arises fast. The notion of inherent existence arises fiercely. The mind has been fabricating the notion of inherent existence since time without beginning. The fierceness of the arising of the notion of inherent existence is the mind's compulsion to fabricate the notion of inherent existence. To detach from the notion of inherent existence is to withstand the fierceness of the arising of the notion of inherent existence. To detach from the notion of inherent existence is to oppose the mind's compulsion to fabricate the notion of inherent existence.

## A continuation of notions

The notion of an entity forms and ceases from moment to moment. A notion of an entity that was is followed by a notion of an entity that is. A notion of an entity that is is followed by a notion of an entity that will be. The notion of an entity is a continuation of notions. To detach from the notion of an entity is to detach from a continuation of notions. To detach from the notion of an entity is to discontinue from moment to moment the formation of each notion of an entity.

## A continuation of notions

The notion of inherent existence forms and ceases from moment to moment. A notion of inherent existence that was is followed by a notion of inherent existence that is. A notion of inherent existence that is is followed by a notion of inherent existence that will be. The notion of inherent existence is a continuation of notions. To detach from the notion of inherent existence is to detach from a continuation of notions. To detach from the notion of inherent existence is to discontinue from moment to moment the formation of each notion of inherent existence.

**Endurance**

The notion of an entity forms and ceases from moment to moment. The notion of an entity is a continuation of notions. Each notion of an entity insists on its arising. Each notion of an entity arises fiercely. The fierceness of the arising of the notion of an entity is the mind's compulsion to fabricate the notion of an entity. To detach from the notion of an entity is to discontinue from moment to moment the formation of each notion of an entity. To detach from the notion of an entity is to withstand from moment to moment the fierceness of the arising of each notion of an entity. To discontinue from moment to moment the formation of each notion of an entity is to endure patiently the absence of the notion of an entity. To withstand from moment to moment the fierceness of the arising of each notion of an entity is to endure patiently the absence of the notion of an entity. Endurance is patient endurance of the absence of the notion of an entity. Endurance is patient endurance of the absence of a continuation of notions.


**Endurance**

The notion of inherent existence forms and ceases from moment to moment. The notion of inherent existence is a continuation of notions. Each notion of inherent existence insists on its arising. Each notion of inherent existence arises fiercely. The fierceness of the arising of the notion of inherent existence is the mind's compulsion to fabricate the notion of inherent existence. To detach from the notion of inherent existence is to discontinue from moment to moment the formation of each notion of inherent existence. To detach from the notion of inherent existence is to withstand from moment to moment the fierceness of the arising of each notion of inherent existence. To discontinue from moment to moment the formation of each notion of inherent existence is to endure patiently the absence of the notion of inherent existence. To withstand from moment to moment the fierceness of the arising of each notion of inherent existence is to endure patiently the absence of the notion of inherent existence. Endurance is patient endurance of the absence of the notion of inherent existence. Endurance is patient endurance of the absence of a continuation of notions.

### Two notions

To detach from the notion of an entity is to detach from the notion of inherent existence. To detach from the notion of an entity is to detach from both the notion of an entity and the notion of inherent existence. To withstand the fierceness of the notion of an entity is to withstand the fierceness of the notion of inherent existence. To withstand the fierceness of the notion of an entity is to withstand both the fierceness of the notion of an entity and the fierceness of the notion of inherent existence. To detach from one is to detach from the other. To detach from one is to detach from both.

### Two notions

To detach from the notion of inherent existence is to detach from the notion of an entity. To detach from the notion of inherent existence is to detach from both the notion of inherent existence and the notion of an entity. To withstand the fierceness of the notion of inherent existence is to withstand the fierceness of the notion of an entity. To withstand the fierceness of the notion of inherent existence is to withstand both the fierceness of the notion of inherent existence and the fierceness of the notion of an entity. To detach from one is to detach from the other. To detach from one is to detach from both.

## Cease the coming together

The notion of an entity comes into being by way of thinking. Thinking is the coming together of the mind, the notion of an entity, and the consciousness of the mind. The mind constitutes the sixth sense. The notion of an entity pertains to the sixth sense object. The consciousness of the mind constitutes the sixth sense consciousness. To detach from the notion of an entity is to cease the coming together of the mind, the notion of an entity, and the consciousness of the mind. To discontinue the formation of the notion of an entity is to discontinue the coming together of the mind, the notion of an entity, and the consciousness of the mind. To endure patiently the absence of the notion of an entity is to endure patiently the absence of the coming together of the mind, the notion of an entity, and the consciousness of the mind.

## Cease the coming together

The notion of inherent existence comes into being by way of thinking. Thinking is the coming together of the mind, the notion of inherent existence, and the consciousness of the mind. The mind constitutes the sixth sense. The notion of inherent existence pertains to the sixth sense object. The consciousness of the mind constitutes the sixth sense consciousness. To detach from the notion of inherent existence is to cease the coming together of the mind, the notion of inherent existence, and the consciousness of the mind. To discontinue the formation of the notion of inherent existence is to discontinue the coming together of the mind, the notion of inherent existence, and the consciousness of the mind. To endure patiently the absence of the notion of inherent existence is to endure patiently the absence of the coming together of the mind, the notion of inherent existence, and the consciousness of the mind.

**The meaning of all buddhas**

The Diamond Sutra says, "To detach from and give up all notions is the meaning of all buddhas." The word 'notion' refers to that which causes the perception of entities. That which causes the perception of entities are notions of entities. The word 'notion' also refers to that which causes the perception of inherent existence. That which causes the perception of inherent existence is the notion of inherent existence. To detach from and give up all notions is to detach from the notion of inherent existence and all notions of entities. Detachment from the notion of inherent existence and all notions of entities is the meaning of all buddhas.

# Detachment

### Forest

A forest is empty and fundamentally absent. The emptiness and fundamental absence of a forest are the true nature of a forest. The emptiness and fundamental absence of a forest are revealed in the absence of the notion of a forest and the absence of the notion of inherent existence. The absence of the notion of a forest and the absence of the notion of inherent existence are arrived at by detaching from the notion of a forest.

To detach from the notion of a forest is to discontinue the formation of the notion of a forest. To detach from the notion of a forest is to seek the immediate absence of the notion of a forest. To detach from the notion of a forest is to withstand the fierceness of the arising of the notion of a forest. To detach from the notion of a forest is to endure patiently the absence of the notion of a forest.

### Mountain

A mountain is empty and fundamentally absent. The emptiness and fundamental absence of a mountain are the true nature of a mountain. The emptiness and fundamental absence of a mountain are revealed in the absence of the notion of a mountain and the absence of the notion of inherent existence. The absence of the notion of a mountain and the absence of the notion of inherent existence are arrived at by detaching from the notion of a mountain.

To detach from the notion of a mountain is to discontinue the formation of the notion of a mountain. To detach from the notion of a mountain is to seek the immediate absence of the notion of a mountain. To detach from the notion of a mountain is to withstand the fierceness of the arising of the notion of a mountain. To detach from the notion of a mountain is to endure patiently the absence of the notion of a mountain.

**River**

A river is empty and fundamentally absent. The emptiness and fundamental absence of a river are the true nature of a river. The emptiness and fundamental absence of a river are revealed in the absence of the notion of a river and the absence of the notion of inherent existence. The absence of the notion of a river and the absence of the notion of inherent existence are arrived at by detaching from the notion of a river.

To detach from the notion of a river is to discontinue the formation of the notion of a river. To detach from the notion of a river is to seek the immediate absence of the notion of a river. To detach from the notion of a river is to withstand the fierceness of the arising of the notion of a river. To detach from the notion of a river is to endure patiently the absence of the notion of a river.

# Detachment in the dust of form

## Detachment from the notion of an entity

The mind perceives the presence of entities in the dust of form. Form is that which is perceived by the eyes. The eyes come together with form and the mind gives rise to the notion of an entity. The coming together of the eyes, form, and the consciousness of the eyes conditions the coming together of the mind, the notion of an entity, and the consciousness of the mind. Seeing conditions thinking. The notion of an entity arises in the presence of form. The presence of the notion of an entity causes the perception of a truly existent entity.

The mind falsely believes that form perceived by the eyes and the notion of an entity fabricated by the mind are one and the same. The mind perceives the presence of an entity in the dust of form. Entities, however, have never existed in the dust of form. All is devoid of entities. Form is devoid of entities. Entities have never come into existence. Entities are fundamentally absent. That which is perceived by the eyes is ungraspable and inexpressible. Form is ungraspable and inexpressible.

The fundamental absence of an entity is revealed by detaching from the notion of an entity. To detach from the notion of an entity is to discontinue the formation of the notion of an entity while the eyes are perceiving form. To detach from the notion of an entity is to cease the coming together of the mind, the notion of an entity, and the consciousness of the mind conditioned by the coming together of the eyes, form, and the consciousness of the eyes. To detach from notions of entities arising in the presence of form is to reveal that form is devoid of entities.

## One and the same

The eyes are not the mind. The first sense is not the sixth sense. Form is not a notion. The first sense object is not the sixth sense object. The mind yet falsely believes that form perceived by the eyes and the notion of an entity fabricated by the mind are one and the same.

### Detachment from the notion of inherent existence

The mind perceives the presence of inherent existence in the dust of form. Form is that which is perceived by the eyes. The eyes come together with form and the mind gives rise to the notion of inherent existence. The coming together of the eyes, form, and the consciousness of the eyes conditions the coming together of the mind, the notion of inherent existence, and the consciousness of the mind. Seeing conditions thinking. The notion of inherent existence arises in the presence of form. The presence of the notion of inherent existence causes the perception of inherent existence.

The mind falsely believes that form perceived by the eyes and the notion of inherent existence fabricated by the mind are one and the same. The mind perceives the presence of inherent existence in the dust of form. The dust of form, however, is devoid of inherent existence. All is devoid of inherent existence. Form is devoid of inherent existence. Inherent existence has never come into being. Inherent existence is fundamentally absent. That which is perceived by the eyes is ungraspable and inexpressible. Form is ungraspable and inexpressible.

The absence of inherent existence is revealed by detaching from the notion of inherent existence. To detach from the notion of inherent existence is to discontinue the formation of the notion of inherent existence while the eyes are perceiving form. To detach from the notion of inherent existence is to cease the coming together of the mind, the notion of inherent existence, and the consciousness of the mind conditioned by the coming together of the eyes, form, and the consciousness of the eyes. To detach from the notion of inherent existence arising in the presence of form is to reveal that form is devoid of inherent existence.

### One and the same

The eyes are not the mind. The first sense is not the sixth sense. Form is not a notion. The first sense object is not the sixth sense object. The mind yet falsely believes that form perceived by the eyes and the notion of inherent existence fabricated by the mind are one and the same.

### Forest

The mind perceives the presence of a forest, when the eyes see a large group of trees. The eyes come together with form of green and brown colors and the mind gives rise to the notion of a forest. The coming together of the eyes, form of green and brown colors, and the consciousness of the eyes conditions the coming together of the mind, the notion of a forest, and the consciousness of the mind. Seeing conditions thinking. The notion of a forest arises in the presence of form. The presence of the notion of a forest causes the perception of a truly existent forest.

The mind falsely believes that form of green and brown colors perceived by the eyes and the notion of a forest fabricated by the mind are one and the same. The mind perceives the presence of a forest in the dust of form. A forest, however, has never existed in the dust of form. Form is devoid of entities. Form is devoid of a forest. A forest has never come into existence. A forest is fundamentally absent. That which is perceived by the eyes is ungraspable and inexpressible. Form of green and brown colors is ungraspable and inexpressible.

The fundamental absence of a forest is revealed by detaching from the notion of a forest. To detach from the notion of a forest is to discontinue the formation of the notion of a forest while the eyes are perceiving form. To detach from the notion of a forest is to cease the coming together of the mind, the notion of a forest, and the consciousness of the mind conditioned by the coming together of the eyes, form of green and brown colors, and the consciousness of the eyes. To detach from the notion of a forest arising in the presence of form is to reveal that form is devoid of a forest.

## Mountain

The mind perceives the presence of a mountain, when the eyes see landform in a certain size and shape. The eyes come together with form of various colors and the mind gives rise to the notion of a mountain. The coming together of the eyes, form, and the consciousness of the eyes conditions the coming together of the mind, the notion of a mountain, and the consciousness of the mind. Seeing conditions thinking. The notion of a mountain arises in the presence of form. The presence of the notion of a mountain causes the perception of a truly existent mountain.

The mind falsely believes that form perceived by the eyes and the notion of a mountain fabricated by the mind are one and the same. The mind perceives the presence of a mountain in the dust of form. A mountain, however, has never existed in the dust of form. Form is devoid of entities. Form is devoid of a mountain. A mountain has never come into existence. A mountain is fundamentally absent. That which is perceived by the eyes is ungraspable and inexpressible. Form is ungraspable and inexpressible.

The fundamental absence of a mountain is revealed by detaching from the notion of a mountain. To detach from the notion of a mountain is to discontinue the formation of the notion of a mountain while the eyes are perceiving form. To detach from the notion of a mountain is to cease the coming together of the mind, the notion of a mountain, and the consciousness of the mind conditioned by the coming together of the eyes, form, and the consciousness of the eyes. To detach from the notion of a mountain arising in the presence of form is to reveal that form is devoid of a mountain.

### River

The mind perceives the presence of a river, when the eyes see masses of water flowing in one direction. The eyes come together with form of blue colors and the mind gives rise to the notion of a river. The coming together of the eyes, form of blue colors, and the consciousness of the eyes conditions the coming together of the mind, the notion of a river, and the consciousness of the mind. Seeing conditions thinking. The notion of a river arises in the presence of form. The presence of the notion of a river causes the perception of a truly existent river.

The mind falsely believes that form of blue colors perceived by the eyes and the notion of a river fabricated by the mind are one and the same. The mind perceives the presence of a river in the dust of form. A river, however, has never existed in the dust of form. Form is devoid of entities. Form is devoid of a river. A river has never come into existence. A river is fundamentally absent. That which is perceived by the eyes is ungraspable and inexpressible. Form of blue colors is ungraspable and inexpressible.

The fundamental absence of a river is revealed by detaching from the notion of a river. To detach from the notion of a river is to discontinue the formation of the notion of a river while the eyes are perceiving form. To detach from the notion of a river is to cease the coming together of the mind, the notion of a river, and the consciousness of the mind conditioned by the coming together of the eyes, form of blue colors, and the consciousness of the eyes. To detach from the notion of a river arising in the presence of form is to reveal that form is devoid of a river.

# The emptiness of a tree and garden

## The emptiness of a tree

The mind perceives the presence of entities. The mind perceives the presence of a tree. A tree is an entity. A tree perceived by the mind is perceived to be endowed with inherent existence. To perceive a tree to be endowed with inherent existence is to perceive a tree to exist independently from everything else. To perceive a tree to be endowed with inherent existence is to perceive a tree as a separate and distinct entity. A tree is a tree endowed with inherent existence. A tree and the inherent existence indwelling in a tree are inseparable.

A tree is devoid of inherent existence. A tree is a composition of roots, a trunk, branches, and leaves. That which is composed of roots, a trunk, branches, and leaves is dependent on roots, a trunk, branches, and leaves. That which is dependent on roots, a trunk, branches, and leaves cannot exist independently from roots, a trunk, branches, and leaves. That which cannot exist independently from roots, a trunk, branches, and leaves cannot exist independently from everything else. That which cannot exist independently from everything else cannot be endowed with inherent existence. That which cannot be endowed with inherent existence is devoid of inherent existence. A tree is devoid of inherent existence.

A tree is fundamentally absent. A tree is a composition of roots, a trunk, branches, and leaves. Roots, a trunk, branches, and leaves cannot constitute a tree. Roots, a trunk, branches, and leaves cannot constitute a composition. A root can only constitute a root. A root can only constitute itself. A leaf can only constitute a leaf. A leaf can only constitute itself. Roots, a trunk, branches, and leaves do not come together and declare to constitute a tree. They do not come together and declare to constitute an entity. A tree has never come into existence. A tree is fundamentally absent. A tree is not a tree, because it is a composition. A tree is a composition and therefore not a tree.

A tree is empty. A tree is devoid of inherent existence. The emptiness of a tree is the absence of inherent existence a tree is perceived to be endowed with. From the absence of inherent existence indwelling in a tree follows the absence of a tree. From the emptiness of a tree follows the fundamental absence of a tree. A tree is fundamentally absent. A tree has never come into existence. That which is fundamentally absent is not. A tree is not. A tree is not a tree. That which is fundamentally absent is inexpressible. A tree is inexpressible. The emptiness and fundamental absence of a tree are the true nature of a tree.

All is mind. A tree perceived by the mind is the notion of a tree fabricated by the mind. Inherent existence a tree is perceived to be endowed with is the notion of inherent existence fabricated by the mind. The presence of the notion of a tree and the presence of the notion of inherent existence cause the perception of an inherently existent tree. It is by way of the notion of inherent existence that a tree is perceived to exist independently from everything else. It is by way of the notion of inherent existence that a tree is perceived as a separate and distinct entity. The fierceness of the arising of the notion of a tree is the mind's compulsion to fabricate the notion of a tree.

The notion of a tree arises in the presence of form. The mind perceives the presence of a tree, when the eyes see a trunk, branches, and leaves. The eyes come together with form of green and brown colors and the mind gives rise to the notion of a tree. The coming together of the eyes, form of green and brown colors, and the consciousness of the eyes conditions the coming together of the mind, the notion of a tree, and the consciousness of the mind. Seeing conditions thinking. The notion of a tree arises in the presence of form. The presence of the notion of a tree causes the perception of a truly existent tree.

The mind falsely believes that form perceived by the eyes and the notion of a tree fabricated by the mind are one and the same. The mind perceives the presence of a tree in the dust of form. A tree, however, has never existed in the dust of form. Form is devoid of entities. Form is devoid of a tree. A tree has never come into existence. A tree is fundamentally absent. That which is perceived by the eyes is ungraspable and inexpressible. Form of green and brown colors is ungraspable and inexpressible.

The emptiness and fundamental absence of a tree are revealed in the absence of the notion of a tree and the absence of the notion of inherent existence. The absence of the notion of a tree and the absence of the notion of inherent existence are the absence of a tree perceived to exist inherently and the absence of inherent existence a tree is perceived to be endowed with. The absence of inherent existence a tree is perceived to be endowed with is the emptiness of a tree.

The absence of the notion of a tree and the absence of the notion of inherent existence are arrived at by detaching from the notion of a tree. To detach from the notion of a tree is to not entertain the notion of a tree. To detach from the notion of a tree is to seek the immediate absence of the notion of a tree. To detach from the notion of a tree is to withstand the fierceness of the arising of the notion of a tree. To detach from the notion of a tree is to endure patiently the absence of the notion of a tree.

To detach from the notion of a tree is to discontinue the formation of the notion of a tree while the eyes are perceiving form of green and brown colors. To detach from the notion of a tree is to cease the coming together of the mind, the notion of a tree, and the consciousness of the mind conditioned by the coming together of the eyes, form of green and brown colors, and the consciousness of the eyes. To detach from the notion of a tree arising in the presence of form is to reveal that form is devoid of a tree.

### The emptiness of a garden

The mind perceives the presence of entities. The mind perceives the presence of a garden. A garden is an entity. A garden perceived by the mind is perceived to be endowed with inherent existence. To perceive a garden to be endowed with inherent existence is to perceive a garden to exist independently from everything else. To perceive a garden to be endowed with inherent existence is to perceive a garden to exist by itself and in itself. A garden is a garden endowed with inherent existence. A garden and the inherent existence indwelling in a garden are inseparable.

A garden is devoid of inherent existence. A garden is a composition of flowers, trees, and ponds. That which is composed of flowers, trees, and ponds is dependent on flowers, trees, and ponds. That which is dependent on flowers, trees, and ponds cannot exist independently from flowers, trees, and ponds. That which cannot exist independently from flowers, trees, and ponds cannot exist independently from everything else. That which cannot exist independently from everything else cannot be endowed with inherent existence. That which cannot be endowed with inherent existence is devoid of inherent existence. A garden is devoid of inherent existence.

A garden is fundamentally absent. A garden is a composition of flowers, trees, and ponds. Flowers, trees, and ponds cannot constitute a garden. Flowers, trees, and ponds cannot constitute a composition. A flower can only constitute a flower. A flower can only constitute itself. A tree can only constitute a tree. A tree can only constitute itself. A pond can only constitute a pond. A pond can only constitute itself. Flowers, trees, and ponds do not come together and declare to constitute a garden. They do not come together and declare to constitute an entity. A garden has never come into existence. A garden is fundamentally absent. A garden is not a garden, because it is a composition. A garden is a composition and therefore not a garden.

A garden is empty. A garden is devoid of inherent existence. The emptiness of a garden is the absence of inherent existence a garden is perceived to be endowed with. From the absence of inherent existence indwelling in a garden follows the absence of a garden. From the emptiness of a garden follows the fundamental absence of a garden. A garden is fundamentally absent. A garden has never come into existence. That which is fundamentally absent is not. A garden is not. A garden is not a garden. That which is fundamentally absent is inexpressible. A garden is inexpressible. The emptiness and fundamental absence of a garden are the true nature of a garden.

All is mind. A garden perceived by the mind is the notion of a garden fabricated by the mind. Inherent existence a garden is perceived to be endowed with is the notion of inherent existence fabricated by the mind. The presence of the notion of a garden and the presence of the notion of inherent existence cause the perception of an inherently existent garden. It is by way of the notion of inherent existence that a garden is perceived to exist independently from everything else. It is by way of the notion of inherent existence that a garden is perceived to exist by itself and in itself. The fierceness of the arising of the notion of a garden is the mind's compulsion to fabricate the notion of a garden.

The notion of a garden arises in the presence of form. The mind perceives the presence of a garden, when the eyes see flowers, trees, and ponds in a certain arrangement. The eyes come together with form of all kinds of colors and the mind gives rise to the notion of a garden. The coming together of the eyes, form of all kinds of colors, and the consciousness of the eyes conditions the coming together of the mind, the notion of a garden, and the consciousness of the mind. Seeing conditions thinking. The notion of a garden arises in the presence of form. The presence of the notion of a garden causes the perception of a truly existent garden.

The mind falsely believes that form perceived by the eyes and the notion of a garden fabricated by the mind are one and the same. The mind perceives the presence of a garden in the dust of form. A garden, however, has never existed in the dust of form. Form is devoid of entities. Form is devoid of a garden. A garden has never come into existence. A garden is fundamentally absent. That which is perceived by the eyes is ungraspable and inexpressible. Form is ungraspable and inexpressible.

The emptiness and fundamental absence of a garden are revealed in the absence of the notion of a garden and the absence of the notion of inherent existence. The absence of the notion of a garden and the absence of the notion of inherent existence are the absence of a garden perceived to exist inherently and the absence of inherent existence a garden is perceived to be endowed with. The absence of inherent existence a garden is perceived to be endowed with is the emptiness of a garden.

The absence of the notion of a garden and the absence of the notion of inherent existence are arrived at by detaching from the notion of a garden. To detach from the notion of a garden is to not entertain the notion of a garden. To detach from the notion of a garden is to seek the immediate absence of the notion of a garden. To detach from the notion of a garden is to withstand the fierceness of the arising of the notion of a garden. To detach from the notion of a garden is to endure patiently the absence of the notion of a garden.

To detach from the notion of a garden is to discontinue the formation of the notion of a garden while the eyes are perceiving form of all kinds of colors. To detach from the notion of a garden is to cease the coming together of the mind, the notion of a garden, and the consciousness of the mind conditioned by the coming together of the eyes, form of all kinds of colors, and the consciousness of the eyes. To detach from the notion of a garden arising in the presence of form is to reveal that form is devoid of a garden.

# Detachment in the five dusts

### Detachment in the dust of form

Notions of entities arise in the presence of form. Form is that which is perceived by the eyes. The eyes come together with form and the mind gives rise to notions of entities. To cultivate detachment in the dust of form is to cease the formation of notions of entities while the eyes are perceiving form. To cultivate detachment in the dust of form is to reveal that form is devoid of entities.

The notion of inherent existence arises in the presence of form. Form is that which is perceived by the eyes. The eyes come together with form and the mind gives rise to the notion of inherent existence. To cultivate detachment in the dust of form is to cease the formation of the notion of inherent existence while the eyes are perceiving form. To cultivate detachment in the dust of form is to reveal that form is devoid of inherent existence.

### Detachment in the dust of sound

Notions of entities arise in the presence of sound. Sound is that which is perceived by the ears. The ears come together with sound and the mind gives rise to notions of entities. To cultivate detachment in the dust of sound is to cease the formation of notions of entities while the ears are perceiving sound. To cultivate detachment in the dust of sound is to reveal that sound is devoid of entities.

The notion of inherent existence arises in the presence of sound. Sound is that which is perceived by the ears. The ears come together with sound and the mind gives rise to the notion of inherent existence. To cultivate detachment in the dust of sound is to cease the formation of the notion of inherent existence while the ears are perceiving sound. To cultivate detachment in the dust of sound is to reveal that sound is devoid of inherent existence.

### Detachment in the dust of smell

Notions of entities arise in the presence of smell. Smell is that which is perceived by the nose. The nose comes together with smell and the mind gives rise to notions of entities. To cultivate detachment in the dust of smell is to cease the formation of notions of entities while the nose is perceiving smell. To cultivate detachment in the dust of smell is to reveal that smell is devoid of entities.

The notion of inherent existence arises in the presence of smell. Smell is that which is perceived by the nose. The nose comes together with smell and the mind gives rise to the notion of inherent existence. To cultivate detachment in the dust of smell is to cease the formation of the notion of inherent existence while the nose is perceiving smell. To cultivate detachment in the dust of smell is to reveal that smell is devoid of inherent existence.

### Detachment in the dust of taste

Notions of entities arise in the presence of taste. Taste is that which is perceived by the tongue. The tongue comes together with taste and the mind gives rise to notions of entities. To cultivate detachment in the dust of taste is to cease the formation of notions of entities while the tongue is perceiving taste. To cultivate detachment in the dust of taste is to reveal that taste is devoid of entities.

The notion of inherent existence arises in the presence of taste. Taste is that which is perceived by the tongue. The tongue comes together with taste and the mind gives rise to the notion of inherent existence. To cultivate detachment in the dust of taste is to cease the formation of the notion of inherent existence while the tongue is perceiving taste. To cultivate detachment in the dust of taste is to reveal that taste is devoid of inherent existence.

**Detachment in the dust of touch**

Notions of entities arise in the presence of touch. Touch is that which is perceived by the body. The body comes together with touch and the mind gives rise to notions of entities. To cultivate detachment in the dust of touch is to cease the formation of notions of entities while the body comes together with touch. To cultivate detachment in the dust of touch is to reveal that touch is devoid of entities.

The notion of inherent existence arises in the presence of touch. Touch is that which is perceived by the body. The body comes together with touch and the mind gives rise to the notion of inherent existence. To cultivate detachment in the dust of touch is to cease the formation of the notion of inherent existence while the body comes together with touch. To cultivate detachment in the dust of touch is to reveal that touch is devoid of inherent existence.

# The three essentials

## Detachment

The emptiness and fundamental absence of an entity are revealed in the absence of the notion of an entity and the absence of the notion of inherent existence.

The absence of the notion of an entity and the absence of the notion of inherent existence can be arrived at by detaching from the notion of an entity.

The absence of the notion of an entity and the absence of the notion of inherent existence can also be arrived at by detaching from the notion of inherent existence.

## The three essentials

The three essentials for cultivating detachment from the notion of an entity are mindfulness, awareness, and endurance. Mindfulness is presence of mind. Mindfulness is the foundation of the way. Awareness is awareness of the presence of the notion of an entity. To be aware of the notion of an entity is to be aware of that which causes the perception of a truly existent entity. To be aware of the notion of an entity is to be aware of that the mind seeks to detach from. Endurance is patient endurance of the absence of the notion of an entity. To withstand from moment to moment the fierceness of the arising of the notion of an entity is to endure patiently the absence of the notion of an entity. Mindfulness, awareness, and endurance are the three essentials for cultivating detachment from the notion of an entity.

**The three essentials**

The three essentials for cultivating detachment from the notion of inherent existence are mindfulness, awareness, and endurance. Mindfulness is presence of mind. Mindfulness is the foundation of the way. Awareness is awareness of the presence of the notion of inherent existence. To be aware of the notion of inherent existence is to be aware of that which causes the perception of inherent existence. To be aware of the notion of inherent existence is to be aware of that the mind seeks to detach from. Endurance is patient endurance of the absence of the notion of inherent existence. To withstand from moment to moment the fierceness of the arising of the notion of inherent existence is to endure patiently the absence of the notion of inherent existence. Mindfulness, awareness, and endurance are the three essentials for cultivating detachment from the notion of inherent existence.

# Mindfulness

## Mindfulness

Mindfulness, awareness, and endurance are the three essentials for cultivating detachment from the notion of an entity and the notion of inherent existence. Mindfulness is the first essential. Mindfulness is presence of mind. To be mindful is to be mindful of the presence of a sense object.

To be mindful is to be mindful of form. Form is the first sense object. Form is that which is perceived by the eyes. To be mindful of form is to be aware that the eyes are perceiving. To be mindful of form is to be aware that seeing takes place.

To be mindful is to be mindful of sound. Sound is the second sense object. Sound is that which is perceived by the ears. To be mindful of sound is to be aware that the ears are perceiving. To be mindful of sound is to be aware that hearing takes place.

To be mindful is to be mindful of touch. Touch is the fifth sense object. Touch is that which is perceived by the body. To be mindful of touch is to be aware that the body is perceiving. To be mindful of touch is to be aware that feeling takes place.

To be mindful is to be mindful of notions. Notions are the sixth sense object. Notions are that which is perceived by the mind. To be mindful of notions is to be aware that the mind is perceiving. To be mindful of notions is to be aware that thinking and feeling take place.

## Sitting meditation

The foremost way to cultivate mindfulness is sitting meditation. To sit is to sit upright. To meditate is to be mindful. Mindfulness is presence of mind. To meditate is to be mindful of an object of meditation. To meditate is to be aware and observant of an object of meditation. The purpose of meditating on an object of meditation is to calm the mind and to attain concentration. From moment to moment, the mind is aware of the object of meditation. From moment to moment, the mind is observant of the object of meditation. Whenever the mind is not aware of the object of meditation, it must quickly return to the object of meditation. Whenever the mind is distracted by wandering thoughts, it must quickly return to the object of meditation. The presence of wandering thoughts is the absence of the object of meditation. The presence of wandering thoughts is the absence of mindfulness. To sit is to sit upright. To meditate is to be mindful. The presence of mindfulness is the presence of the way.

### Mindfulness of the Buddha

To sit is to sit upright. To meditate is to be mindful of an object of meditation. Such an object of meditation is the name of the Buddha. To be mindful of the Buddha is to think of the name of the Buddha. To be mindful of the Buddha is to uninterruptedly bring to mind the name of the Buddha. The name of the Buddha is Shakyamuni Buddha. To be mindful of the Buddha is to uninterruptedly bring to mind the words, "Namo Shakyamuni Buddha, Namo Shakyamuni Buddha, Namo Shakyamuni Buddha, Namo Shakyamuni Buddha." The word 'namo' is Sanskrit and means 'veneration' or 'obeisance'. From moment to moment, the mind is aware of the name of the Buddha. From moment to moment, the mind is observant of the name of the Buddha. Whenever the mind does not think of the name of the Buddha, it must quickly return to the name of the Buddha. Whenever the mind is distracted by wandering thoughts, it must quickly return to the name of the Buddha. The presence of wandering thoughts is the absence of the name of the Buddha. The presence of wandering thoughts is the absence of mindfulness. To meditate is to be mindful of an object of meditation. The name of the Buddha in any language is such an object of meditation. To meditate is to meditate without haste. To be mindful of the Buddha is to be mindful of the sixth sense object. Notions are the sixth sense object. Thinking is the coming together of the mind, the name of the Buddha, and the consciousness of the mind. To sit is to sit upright. To meditate is to be mindful. The presence of mindfulness is the presence of the way.

### Wandering thoughts

Mindfulness is presence of mind. Mindfulness is the foundation of the way. The absence of mindfulness is the absence of the way. The absence of mindfulness can be caused by the presence of wandering thoughts. Wandering thoughts arise from the mind. The mind is that which gives rise to wandering thoughts. Wandering thoughts pertain to the sixth sense object. Notions are the sixth sense object. The mind that is wallowing in wandering thoughts is not aware that it is wallowing in wandering thoughts. The mind that is carried away by wandering thoughts is not aware that it is carried away by wandering thoughts. The presence of wandering thoughts is the absence of mindfulness. The presence of wandering thoughts is the absence of the way.

### One notion at a time

The mind that is aware of the name of the Buddha cannot harbor a wandering thought, for the mind can only entertain one notion at a time. The presence of the name of the Buddha is the absence of wandering thoughts. The presence of the name of the Buddha is the presence of mindfulness.

The mind that is wallowing in wandering thoughts cannot be aware of the name of the Buddha, for the mind can only entertain one notion at a time. The presence of wandering thoughts is the absence of the name of the Buddha. The presence of wandering thoughts is the absence of mindfulness.

The absence of wandering thoughts is the presence of mindfulness. The absence of wandering thoughts is arrived at by detaching from wandering thoughts. To return to the name of the Buddha in the presence of wandering thoughts is to detach from wandering thoughts, for the mind can only entertain one notion at a time.

## Taming the mind

To meditate is to calm the scattered mind. To meditate is to cease the scattered mind. The absence of the scattered mind is the presence of mindfulness. The presence of mindfulness is the presence of the way.

To meditate is to calm the restless mind. To meditate is to cease the restless mind. The absence of the restless mind is the presence of mindfulness. The presence of mindfulness is the presence of the way.

To meditate is to calm the wayward mind. To meditate is to cease the wayward mind. The absence of the wayward mind is the presence of mindfulness. The presence of mindfulness is the presence of the way.

To meditate is to calm the unruly mind. To meditate is to cease the unruly mind. The absence of the unruly mind is the presence of mindfulness. The presence of mindfulness is the presence of the way.


## Stilling the mind

To meditate is to calm the mind that is anxious and worried. To meditate is to purify the mind that is anxious and worried. Meditation can still the presence of worry. Meditation can ease the presence of worry.

To meditate is to calm the mind that is afraid and fearful. To meditate is to purify the mind that is afraid and fearful. Meditation can still the presence of fear. Meditation can ease the presence of fear.

To meditate is to calm the mind that is afflicted and vexed. To meditate is to purify the mind that is afflicted and vexed. Meditation can still the presence of vexation. Meditation can ease the presence of vexation.

To meditate is to calm the mind that is anguished and tormented. To meditate is to purify the mind that is anguished and tormented. Meditation can still the presence of anguish. Meditation can ease the presence of anguish.

## Walking, standing, sitting, and lying down

Sitting meditation is the preferred way to calm the mind and to attain concentration. Sitting meditation is the foundation of meditation. Meditation, however, is not restricted to sitting meditation. Meditation is not the posture of the body. Meditation is presence of mind. To meditate is to calm the mind and attain concentration while walking. To meditate is to cultivate mindfulness while walking. To meditate is to calm the mind and attain concentration while standing. To meditate is to cultivate mindfulness while standing. To meditate is to calm the mind and attain concentration while sitting. To meditate is to cultivate mindfulness while sitting. To meditate is to calm the mind and attain concentration while lying down. To meditate is to cultivate mindfulness while lying down. To practice meditation is to calm the mind and attain concentration while walking, standing, sitting, and lying down. To practice meditation is to cultivate mindfulness while walking, standing, sitting, and lying down. Although meditation is not the posture of the body, sitting meditation must never be neglected, because sitting meditation is the foundation of meditation.

## Walking meditation

To practice walking meditation is to be mindful of an object of meditation while walking. From moment to moment, the mind is aware of the object of meditation. From moment to moment, the mind is observant of the object of meditation. Whenever the mind is not aware of the object of meditation, it must quickly return to the object of meditation. Whenever the mind is distracted by wandering thoughts, it must quickly return to the object of meditation. The presence of wandering thoughts is the absence of the object of meditation. The presence of wandering thoughts is the absence of mindfulness.

While the body walks, the eyes see. While the body walks, form is perceived. Seeing is the coming together of the eyes, form, and the consciousness of the eyes. Form can cause the arising of wandering thoughts. Form can cause the absence of mindfulness. The eyes may therefore at first look downward while practicing walking meditation. The eyes may then come together with all kinds of form while practicing walking meditation. To practice walking meditation is to cultivate mindfulness while walking. While the body is moving, the mind remains unmoved. While the body is in motion, the mind remains in stillness.

### Walking meditation

To practice walking meditation is to be mindful of an object of meditation while walking. Such an object of meditation is the name of the Buddha. To be mindful of the Buddha is to think of the name of the Buddha. From moment to moment, the mind is aware of the name of the Buddha. From moment to moment, the mind is observant of the name of the Buddha. The presence of the name of the Buddha is the absence of wandering thoughts, for the mind can only entertain one notion at a time. To be mindful of the name of the Buddha is to be mindful of the sixth sense object. Notions are the sixth sense object. Thinking is the coming together of the mind, the name of the Buddha, and the consciousness of the mind.

To practice walking meditation is to be mindful of an object of meditation while walking. Such an object of meditation is the feeling perceived, when the feet touch the ground while walking. From moment to moment, the mind is observant of that feeling perceived. From moment to moment, the mind is aware of that feeling perceived. To be mindful of one's footsteps is to be mindful of the fifth sense object. Touch is the fifth sense object. Feeling is the coming together of the body, touch, and the consciousness of the body. Mindfulness of touch is the absence of wandering thoughts, for the mind can only perceive one sense object at a time. The absence of wandering thoughts is the presence of mindfulness. The absence of wandering thoughts is the presence of the way.

### In stillness and in motion

To practice meditation is to cultivate mindfulness. Meditation is the cause. Mindfulness is the effect. To practice meditation is to cultivate mindfulness in stillness. Meditation in stillness is the cause. Mindfulness in stillness is the effect. To practice meditation is to cultivate mindfulness in motion. Meditation in motion is the cause. Mindfulness in motion is the effect. To practice meditation is to cultivate mindfulness in the absence of people. Meditation in the absence of people is the cause. Mindfulness in the absence of people is the effect. To practice meditation is to cultivate mindfulness in the presence of people. Meditation in the presence of people is the cause. Mindfulness in the presence of people is the effect. To practice meditation is to cultivate mindfulness in favorable situations. Meditation in favorable situations is the cause. Mindfulness in favorable situations is the effect. To practice meditation is to cultivate mindfulness in adverse situations. Meditation in adverse situations is the cause. Mindfulness in adverse situations is the effect.

### Feelings

To practice meditation is to cultivate mindfulness. Meditation is the cause. Mindfulness is the effect. To practice meditation is to cultivate mindfulness in the presence of desire. Meditation in the presence of desire is the cause. Mindfulness in the presence of desire is the effect. To practice meditation is to cultivate mindfulness in the presence of hatred. Meditation in the presence of hatred is the cause. Mindfulness in the presence of hatred is the effect. To practice meditation is to cultivate mindfulness in the presence of pleasure. Meditation in the presence of pleasure is the cause. Mindfulness in the presence of pleasure is the effect. To practice meditation is to cultivate mindfulness in the presence of suffering. Meditation in the presence of suffering is the cause. Mindfulness in the presence of suffering is the effect.

## Vexation

To be mindful is to be aware of the mind that is anxious and worried. The presence of worry can cause the absence of mindfulness. The absence of mindfulness is the absence of the way. To be mindful is to retain mindfulness in the presence of worry. Mindfulness in the presence of worry is the presence of the way.

To be mindful is to be aware of the mind that is afraid and fearful. The presence of fear can cause the absence of mindfulness. The absence of mindfulness is the absence of the way. To be mindful is to retain mindfulness in the presence of fear. Mindfulness in the presence of fear is the presence of the way.

To be mindful is to be aware of the mind that is afflicted and vexed. The presence of vexation can cause the absence of mindfulness. The absence of mindfulness is the absence of the way. To be mindful is to retain mindfulness in the presence of vexation. Mindfulness in the presence of vexation is the presence of the way.

To be mindful is to be aware of the mind that is anguished and tormented. The presence of anguish can cause the absence of mindfulness. The absence of mindfulness is the absence of the way. To be mindful is to retain mindfulness in the presence of anguish. Mindfulness in the presence of anguish is the presence of the way.

# Awareness and endurance:
# The notion of an entity

## Awareness

Mindfulness, awareness, and endurance are the three essentials for cultivating detachment from the notion of an entity. Awareness is the second essential. Awareness is awareness of the presence of the notion of an entity. An entity perceived by the mind is the notion of an entity fabricated by the mind. To be aware of the notion of an entity is to be aware of that which causes the perception of a truly existent entity. To be aware of the notion of an entity is to be aware of that the mind seeks to detach from.

The notion of an entity arises from the mind. It comes into being by way of thinking. Thinking is the coming together of the mind, the notion of an entity, and the consciousness of the mind. The mind that seeks to be aware of the notion of an entity must seek within itself. The mind must reflect back. To cultivate awareness is to reflect back and to discern the presence of the notion of an entity. To cultivate awareness is to reflect back and to mindfully observe the presence of the notion of an entity. Awareness is essential.

## Awareness

The mind that is dwelling on the notion of an entity is not aware of its dwelling. The mind that is not aware of its dwelling cannot detach from the notion of an entity.

The mind that is dwelling on the notion of an entity must reflect back and be aware of its dwelling. The mind can detach from the notion of an entity only if it is aware of its dwelling.

### Endurance

Mindfulness, awareness, and endurance are the three essentials for cultivating detachment from the notion of an entity. Endurance is the third essential. Endurance is patient endurance of the absence of the notion of an entity. The notion of an entity forms and ceases from moment to moment. The notion of an entity is a succession of notions. The notion of an entity is a continuation of notions. Each notion of an entity insists on its arising. Each notion of an entity arises fiercely. The fierceness of the arising of the notion of an entity is the mind's compulsion to fabricate the notion of an entity. To endure patiently the absence of the notion of an entity is to withstand from moment to moment the fierceness of the arising of the notion of an entity. To endure patiently the absence of the notion of an entity is to oppose from moment to moment the mind's compulsion to fabricate the notion of an entity. Detachment from the notion of an entity is detachment from a continuation of notions. Endurance of the absence of the notion of an entity is endurance of the absence of a continuation of notions. Endurance is essential.

### Mindfulness, awareness, and endurance

Mindfulness, awareness, and endurance are the three essentials for cultivating detachment from the notion of an entity. Mindfulness is presence of mind. Awareness is awareness of the presence of the notion of an entity. Endurance is endurance of the absence of the notion of an entity.

Mindfulness is a precondition for awareness. The first essential is a precondition for the second essential. Awareness is a precondition for endurance. The second essential is a precondition for the third essential. Mindfulness and awareness are preconditions for endurance. The first and second essential are preconditions for the third essential.

Mindfulness is the foundation of the way. Detachment from all notions of entities is the way.

# Awareness and endurance:
# The notion of inherent existence

## Awareness

Mindfulness, awareness, and endurance are the three essentials for cultivating detachment from the notion of inherent existence. Awareness is the second essential. Awareness is awareness of the presence of the notion of inherent existence. Entities perceived by the mind are perceived to be endowed with inherent existence. The perception of inherent existence is caused by the presence of the notion of inherent existence. To be aware of the notion of inherent existence is to be aware of that which causes the perception of inherent existence. To be aware of the notion of inherent existence is to be aware of that the mind seeks to detach from.

The notion of inherent existence arises from the mind. It comes into being by way of thinking. Thinking is the coming together of the mind, the notion of inherent existence, and the consciousness of the mind. The mind that seeks to be aware of the notion of inherent existence must seek within itself. The mind must reflect back. To cultivate awareness is to reflect back and to discern the presence of the notion of inherent existence. To cultivate awareness is to reflect back and to mindfully observe the presence of the notion of inherent existence. Awareness is essential.

## Awareness

The mind that is dwelling on the notion of inherent existence is not aware of its dwelling. The mind that is not aware of its dwelling cannot detach from the notion of inherent existence.

The mind that is dwelling on the notion of inherent existence must reflect back and be aware of its dwelling. The mind can detach from the notion of inherent existence only if it is aware of its dwelling.

### Endurance

Mindfulness, awareness, and endurance are the three essentials for cultivating detachment from the notion of inherent existence. Endurance is the third essential. Endurance is patient endurance of the absence of the notion of inherent existence. The notion of inherent existence forms and ceases from moment to moment. The notion of inherent existence is a succession of notions. The notion of inherent existence is a continuation of notions. Each notion of inherent existence insists on its arising. Each notion of inherent existence arises fiercely. The fierceness of the arising of the notion of inherent existence is the mind's compulsion to fabricate the notion of inherent existence. To endure patiently the absence of the notion of inherent existence is to withstand from moment to moment the fierceness of the arising of the notion of inherent existence. To endure patiently the absence of the notion of inherent existence is to oppose from moment to moment the mind's compulsion to fabricate the notion of inherent existence. Detachment from the notion of inherent existence is detachment from a continuation of notions. Endurance of the absence of the notion of inherent existence is endurance of the absence of a continuation of notions. Endurance is essential.

### Mindfulness, awareness, and endurance

Mindfulness, awareness, and endurance are the three essentials for cultivating detachment from the notion of inherent existence. Mindfulness is presence of mind. Awareness is awareness of the presence of the notion of inherent existence. Endurance is endurance of the absence of the notion of inherent existence.

Mindfulness is a precondition for awareness. The first essential is a precondition for the second essential. Awareness is a precondition for endurance. The second essential is a precondition for the third essential. Mindfulness and awareness are preconditions for endurance. The first and second essential are preconditions for the third essential.

Mindfulness is the foundation of the way. Detachment from the notion of inherent existence is the way.

# The three essentials

## Cultivation

Mindfulness is the first essential to cultivate. Awareness is the second essential to cultivate. Endurance is the third essential to cultivate.

## Meditation

The three essentials for cultivating detachment are mindfulness, awareness, and endurance. All three essentials can be cultivated by practicing meditation. All three essentials can be cultivated by being mindful of an object of meditation. First, to be mindful of an object of meditation is to calm the mind and attain concentration. To calm the mind and attain concentration is to cultivate mindfulness. Mindfulness is the first essential. Second, to be mindful of an object of meditation is to be aware of the presence of wandering thoughts. To be aware of the presence of wandering thoughts is to be aware of that the mind seeks to detach from. To be aware of that the mind seeks to detach from is to cultivate awareness. Awareness is the second essential. Third, to be mindful of an object of meditation is to return to the object of meditation in the presence of wandering thoughts. To return to the object of meditation in the presence of wandering thoughts is to detach from wandering thoughts, for the mind can only perceive one sense object at a time. To detach from wandering thoughts is to endure the absence of wandering thoughts. To endure the absence of wandering thoughts is to cultivate endurance. Endurance is the third essential. To be mindful of an object of meditation is to cultivate mindfulness, awareness, and endurance. Mindfulness is presence of mind. Awareness is awareness of the presence of wandering thoughts. Endurance is endurance of the absence of wandering thoughts. To practice meditation is to cultivate mindfulness, awareness, and endurance.

### In stillness and in motion

Mindfulness is cultivated in stillness and in motion. Mindfulness is cultivated in the absence of people and in the presence of people. Mindfulness is cultivated in favorable situations and in adverse situations.

Awareness is cultivated in stillness and in motion. Awareness is cultivated in the absence of people and in the presence of people. Awareness is cultivated in favorable situations and in adverse situations.

Endurance is cultivated in stillness and in motion. Endurance is cultivated in the absence of people and in the presence of people. Endurance is cultivated in favorable situations and in adverse situations.

# The ability to withstand

### The impenetrableness of notions of entities

The formation of notions of entities is difficult to cease. Notions of entities seem to be impenetrable. The impenetrableness of the notion of an entity stems from the fierceness of the arising of the notion of an entity. The fierceness of the arising of the notion of an entity is the mind's compulsion to fabricate the notion of an entity. To break through the impenetrableness of the notion of an entity, the mind must learn and practice the ability to withstand. To withstand is to withstand the fierceness of the arising of the notion of an entity. The ability to withstand is learned and practiced by cultivating detachment from heaven and earth.

### The impenetrableness of the notion of inherent existence

The formation of the notion of inherent existence is difficult to cease. The notion of inherent existence seems to be impenetrable. The impenetrableness of the notion of inherent existence stems from the fierceness of the arising of the notion of inherent existence. The fierceness of the arising of the notion of inherent existence is the mind's compulsion to fabricate the notion of inherent existence. To break through the impenetrableness of the notion of inherent existence, the mind must learn and practice the ability to withstand. To withstand is to withstand the fierceness of the arising of the notion of inherent existence. The ability to withstand is learned and practiced by cultivating detachment from heaven and earth.

### Heaven and earth

Heaven and earth refer to the entirety of the sixth sense object. Thinking and feeling are the coming together of the mind, notions, and the consciousness of the mind. To detach from heaven and earth is to learn and practice the ability to withstand.

Thoughts and feelings pertain to the sixth sense object. To detach from all thoughts and all feelings is to detach from heaven and earth. To detach from all thoughts and all feelings is to learn and practice the ability to withstand.

Notions of entities pertain to the sixth sense object. To detach from notions of entities is to detach from heaven and earth. To detach from notions of entities is to learn and practice the ability to withstand.

The notion of inherent existence pertains to the sixth sense object. To detach from the notion of inherent existence is to detach from heaven and earth. To detach from the notion of inherent existence is to learn and practice the ability to withstand.


### Feelings

To withstand the fierceness of the arising of desire is to learn and practice the ability to withstand. To endure patiently the absence of desire is to learn and practice the ability to withstand.

To withstand the fierceness of the arising of hatred is to learn and practice the ability to withstand. To endure patiently the absence of hatred is to learn and practice the ability to withstand.

To withstand the fierceness of the arising of arrogance is to learn and practice the ability to withstand. To endure patiently the absence of arrogance is to learn and practice the ability to withstand.

**In stillness and in motion**

Detachment from heaven and earth is cultivated in stillness and in motion. Detachment from heaven and earth is cultivated in the absence of people and in the presence of people. Detachment from heaven and earth is cultivated in favorable situations and in adverse situations.

**Breaking through**

The mind that cultivates detachment from heaven and earth will be able to break through the impenetrableness of all notions of entities.

The mind that cultivates detachment from heaven and earth will be able to break through the impenetrableness of the notion of inherent existence.

# The perfection of wisdom

### Detachment from all notions of entities

The perfection of wisdom is the cultivation of wisdom. Wisdom is understanding the true nature of all. The emptiness and fundamental absence of entities are the true nature of all. The emptiness and fundamental absence of entities are revealed by cultivating detachment from all notions of entities. Wisdom is revealed by cultivating detachment from all notions of entities. To cultivate detachment from all notions of entities is to cultivate the perfection of wisdom. To endure patiently the absence of all notions of entities is to cultivate the perfection of wisdom.

### Detachment from the notion of inherent existence

The perfection of wisdom is the cultivation of wisdom. Wisdom is understanding the true nature of all. The emptiness and fundamental absence of entities are the true nature of all. The emptiness and fundamental absence of entities are revealed by cultivating detachment from the notion of inherent existence. Wisdom is revealed by cultivating detachment from the notion of inherent existence. To cultivate detachment from the notion of inherent existence is to cultivate the perfection of wisdom. To endure patiently the absence of the notion of inherent existence is to cultivate the perfection of wisdom.

# Ignorance and wisdom

### Suffering

Sentient beings suffer in samsara since time without beginning. Suffering has a cause. The afflictions are the cause of suffering. The afflictions are ignorance, desire, and hatred. Suffering can be ceased. Suffering is ceased by ceasing the cause of suffering. Suffering is ceased by ceasing ignorance, desire, and hatred.

Ignorance, desire, and hatred are the cause of suffering. Desire and hatred arise from ignorance. Ignorance gives rise to desire and hatred. Ignorance is the fundamental cause of all suffering. Suffering is ceased by ceasing the fundamental cause of suffering. Suffering is ceased by ceasing the affliction of ignorance.

### Ignorance

Ignorance is the perception of that which is fundamentally absent. Entities are fundamentally absent. All is devoid of entities. Ignorance is the perception of entities.

Ignorance is the perception of that which is fundamentally absent. Inherent existence is fundamentally absent. All is devoid of inherent existence. Ignorance is the perception of inherent existence.

Ignorance is the perception of that which is fundamentally absent. Inherently existent entities are fundamentally absent. Ignorance is the perception of inherently existent entities.

### Cessation of ignorance

Suffering is ceased by ceasing the cause of suffering. Suffering is ceased by ceasing the affliction of ignorance. Ignorance is the perception of inherently existent entities. Suffering is ceased by ceasing the perception of inherently existent entities.

### Detachment

Suffering is ceased by ceasing the perception of inherently existent entities. The perception of inherently existent entities is ceased by cultivating detachment from the notion of inherent existence and all notions of entities.

To cultivate detachment from the notion of inherent existence and all notions of entities is to cease the affliction of ignorance. To cultivate detachment from the notion of inherent existence and all notions of entities is to cease the cause of suffering.

### The perfection of wisdom

The perfection of wisdom is detachment from the notion of inherent existence. The perfection of wisdom is detachment from all notions of entities. To cultivate detachment from the notion of inherent existence and all notions of entities is to cultivate the perfection of wisdom.

Suffering is ceased by ceasing the perception of inherently existent entities. The perception of inherently existent entities is ceased by cultivating detachment from the notion of inherent existence and all notions of entities. The perception of inherently existent entities is ceased by cultivating the perfection of wisdom.

To cultivate the perfection of wisdom is to cease the affliction of ignorance. To cultivate the perfection of wisdom is to cease the fundamental cause of suffering. Unsurpassed complete enlightenment is attained by cultivating the perfection of wisdom.

# The emptiness of the self

### The self

The mind perceives the presence of entities. The mind perceives the presence of a self. The self is an entity. The self perceived by the mind is perceived to be endowed with inherent existence. To perceive the self to be endowed with inherent existence is to perceive the self to exist independently from everything else. To perceive the self to be endowed with inherent existence is to perceive the self as a separate and distinct entity. The self is a self endowed with inherent existence. The self and the inherent existence indwelling in the self are inseparable.

### The emptiness of the self

The self is empty. The self is devoid of inherent existence. The emptiness of the self is the absence of inherent existence the self is perceived to be endowed with. The emptiness of the self is the true nature of the self. The absence of inherent existence is the true nature of the self.

### The emptiness of the self

The self is empty. The self is devoid of inherent existence. The self is composed of the five skandhas. The self is a composition of the five skandhas. The five skandhas are form, feeling, thinking, volition, and consciousness. Form constitutes the body. Feeling, thinking, volition, and consciousness constitute the mind. The self is composed of the five skandhas. That which is composed of the five skandhas is dependent on the five skandhas. That which is dependent on the five skandhas cannot exist independently from the five skandhas. That which cannot exist independently from the five skandhas cannot exist independently from everything else. That which cannot exist independently from everything else cannot be endowed with inherent existence. That which cannot be endowed with inherent existence is devoid of inherent existence. That which is devoid of inherent existence is empty. The self is devoid of inherent existence. The self is empty. The emptiness of the self is the absence of inherent existence the self is perceived to be endowed with. That which is composed is inevitably empty. The self is composed of form, feeling, thinking, volition, and consciousness and therefore empty. To understand that the self can as a composition not be endowed with inherent existence is to understand the impossibility of the self to be endowed with inherent existence. To understand that the self can as a composition not be endowed with inherent existence is to understand conceptually the emptiness of the self.

### The fundamental absence of the self

The self is fundamentally absent. A self has never come into existence. That which is fundamentally absent is not. The self is not. The self is not a self. That which is fundamentally absent is inexpressible. The self is inexpressible. The fundamental absence of the self is the true nature of the self.

### The fundamental absence of the self

The self is empty. The self is devoid of inherent existence. The emptiness of the self is the absence of inherent existence the self is perceived to be endowed with. From the absence of inherent existence indwelling in the self follows the absence of the self. From the emptiness of the self follows the fundamental absence of the self. A self devoid of inherent existence is not a self. A self devoid of inherent existence is not. The self is fundamentally absent.

### The fundamental absence of the self

The self is fundamentally absent. The self is a composition of the five skandhas. The five skandhas are form, feeling, thinking, volition, and consciousness. Form, feeling, thinking, volition, and consciousness cannot constitute a self. Form, feeling, thinking, volition, and consciousness cannot constitute an entity. A self has never come into existence. The self is fundamentally absent. Compositions have never come into existence. Compositions are fundamentally absent. The self is not a self, because it is a composition. The self is a composition and therefore not a self. To understand conceptually the fundamental absence of the self is to understand conceptually the emptiness of the self.

### The notion of self

The mind perceives the presence of a self. The perception of a self is caused by the presence of the notion of self. The notion of self arises from the mind. The mind is that which gives rise to the notion of self. The notion of self comes into being by way of thinking. Thinking is the coming together of the mind, the notion of self, and the consciousness of the mind. The mind fabricates the notion of self and it mistakes the presence of the notion of self for a truly existent self. The self perceived by the mind is the notion of self fabricated by the mind.

### The notion of inherent existence

The mind perceives the presence of a self. The self perceived by the mind is perceived to be endowed with inherent existence. The perception of inherent existence is caused by the presence of the notion of inherent existence. The notion of inherent existence arises from the mind. The mind is that which gives rise to the notion of inherent existence. The notion of inherent existence comes into being by way of thinking. Thinking is the coming together of the mind, the notion of inherent existence, and the consciousness of the mind. The mind fabricates the notion of inherent existence and it mistakes the presence of the notion of inherent existence for inherent existence. Inherent existence the self is perceived to be endowed with is the notion of inherent existence fabricated by the mind.


### An inherently existent self

The mind perceives an inherently existent self. An inherently existent self is a self endowed with inherent existence. The perception of an inherently existent self is caused by the presence of the notion of self and the presence of the notion of inherent existence. The mind gives rise to the notion of self and the notion of inherent existence and it mistakes the presence of the notion of self and the presence of the notion of inherent existence for an inherently existent self.


### Perception

The mind perceives the presence of a self. A self, however, has never come into existence. The self is fundamentally absent. The mind perceives that which is fundamentally absent. The perception of a self is caused by the presence of the notion of self. The mind gives rise to the notion of self and it mistakes the presence of the notion of self for a truly existent self. The presence of the notion of self causes the perception of a self. The presence of the notion of self causes the perception of that which is fundamentally absent. The mind perceives that which is fundamentally absent, because it fabricates a notion of that which is fundamentally absent.

The self is perceived to be endowed with inherent existence. The self, however, is devoid of inherent existence. All is devoid of inherent existence. Inherent existence is fundamentally absent. The mind perceives that which is devoid of inherent existence to be endowed with inherent existence. The perception of inherent existence is caused by the presence of the notion of inherent existence. The mind gives rise to the notion of inherent existence and it mistakes the presence of the notion of inherent existence for inherent existence. The presence of the notion of inherent existence causes the perception of inherent existence. The mind perceives the self to be endowed with inherent existence, because it fabricates the notion of inherent existence. The mind perceives that which is devoid of inherent existence to be endowed with inherent existence, because it fabricates the notion of inherent existence.

### Revealing the fundamental absence of the self

The self is fundamentally absent. A self has never come into existence. The fundamental absence of the self is the true nature of the self. The fundamental absence of the self is revealed in the absence of the notion of self. The perception of a self is caused by the presence of the notion of self. The perception of a self does not come into being in the absence of the notion of self. The absence of the notion of self is the absence of the perception of a self. The absence of the perception of a self reveals the fundamental absence of the self. The fundamental absence of the self is revealed in the absence of the notion of self.

### Revealing the emptiness of the self

The self is empty. The self is devoid of inherent existence. The emptiness of the self is the absence of inherent existence the self is perceived to be endowed with. The emptiness of the self is revealed in the absence of the notion of inherent existence. The perception of inherent existence is caused by the presence of the notion of inherent existence. The perception of inherent existence does not come into being in the absence of the notion of inherent existence. The absence of the notion of inherent existence is the absence of the perception of inherent existence. The absence of the perception of inherent existence reveals the emptiness of the self. The emptiness of the self is revealed in the absence of the notion of inherent existence.

## Revealing the true nature of the self

The self is empty and fundamentally absent. The emptiness and fundamental absence of the self are the true nature of the self. The emptiness and fundamental absence of the self are revealed in the absence of the notion of self and the absence of the notion of inherent existence. The perception of an inherently existent self is caused by the presence of the notion of self and the presence of the notion of inherent existence. The perception of an inherently existent self does not come into being in the absence of the notion of self and the absence of the notion of inherent existence. The absence of the notion of self and the absence of the notion of inherent existence are the absence of a self perceived to exist inherently and the absence of inherent existence the self is perceived to be endowed with. The absence of inherent existence the self is perceived to be endowed with is the emptiness of the self. The emptiness and fundamental absence of the self are revealed in the absence of the notion of self and the absence of the notion of inherent existence.

## Detachment from the notion of self

The self is empty and fundamentally absent. The emptiness and fundamental absence of the self are revealed in the absence of the notion of self and the absence of the notion of inherent existence. The absence of the notion of self and the absence of the notion of inherent existence are arrived at by detaching from the notion of self. To detach from the notion of self is to not entertain the notion of self. To detach from the notion of self is to discontinue the formation of the notion of self. To detach from the notion of self is to seek the immediate absence of the notion of self. To detach from the notion of self is to withstand the fierceness of the arising of the notion of self. To detach from the notion of self is to endure patiently the absence of the notion of self.

## Detachment from the notion of inherent existence

The self is empty and fundamentally absent. The emptiness and fundamental absence of the self are revealed in the absence of the notion of self and the absence of the notion of inherent existence. The absence of the notion of self and the absence of the notion of inherent existence are arrived at by detaching from the notion of inherent existence. To detach from the notion of inherent existence is to not entertain the notion of inherent existence. To detach from the notion of inherent existence is to discontinue the formation of the notion of inherent existence. To detach from the notion of inherent existence is to seek the immediate absence of the notion of inherent existence. To detach from the notion of inherent existence is to withstand the fierceness of the arising of the notion of inherent existence. To detach from the notion of inherent existence is to endure patiently the absence of the notion of inherent existence.

## The perfection of wisdom

The perfection of wisdom is the cultivation of wisdom. Wisdom is understanding the true nature of all. Wisdom is understanding the true nature of the self. The emptiness and fundamental absence of the self are the true nature of the self. The emptiness and fundamental absence of the self are revealed by cultivating detachment from the notion of self. Wisdom is revealed by cultivating detachment from the notion of self. To cultivate detachment from the notion of self is to cultivate the perfection of wisdom. To endure patiently the absence of the notion of self is to cultivate the perfection of wisdom.

# Detachment from the notion of self

### The three essentials

Detachment is the way. Detachment is detachment from notions of entities. Detachment is detachment from the notion of self. The three essentials for cultivating detachment from the notion of self are mindfulness, awareness, and endurance. Mindfulness is presence of mind. Awareness is awareness of the presence of the notion of self. Endurance is endurance of the absence of the notion of self.

### Mindfulness

Mindfulness is the first essential. Mindfulness is presence of mind. To be mindful is to be mindful of the presence of a sense object. To be mindful is to be mindful of form, sound, touch, or notions. Mindfulness is the foundation of the way. The absence of mindfulness is the absence of the way.

### Awareness

Awareness is the second essential. Awareness is awareness of the presence of the notion of self. The self perceived by the mind is the notion of self fabricated by the mind. To be aware of the notion of self is to be aware of that which causes the perception of a truly existent self. To be aware of the notion of self is to be aware of that the mind seeks to detach from.

The notion of self arises from the mind. It comes into being by way of thinking. The mind that seeks awareness of the notion of self must seek within itself. The mind must reflect back. To cultivate awareness is to reflect back and to discern the presence of the notion of self. To cultivate awareness is to reflect back and to mindfully observe the presence of the notion of self.

## Awareness

The mind that is dwelling on the notion of self is not aware of its dwelling. The mind that is not aware of its dwelling cannot detach from the notion of self.

The mind that is dwelling on the notion of self must reflect back and be aware of its dwelling. The mind can detach from the notion of self only if it is aware of its dwelling.


## Awareness

The mind is constantly entertaining the notion of self. Awareness of the notion of self is awareness of that which is constantly being entertained.


## Endurance

Endurance is the third essential. Endurance is patient endurance of the absence of the notion of self. The notion of self forms and ceases from moment to moment. A notion of self that was is followed by a notion of self that is. A notion of self that is is followed by a notion of self that will be. The notion of self is an unending succession of notions. The notion of self is an unending continuation of notions. Each notion of self insists on its arising. Each notion of self arises fiercely. The fierceness of the arising of the notion of self is the mind's incessant compulsion to fabricate the notion of self. To endure patiently the absence of the notion of self is to withstand from moment to moment the fierceness of the arising of the notion of self. To endure patiently the absence of the notion of self is to oppose from moment to moment the mind's compulsion to fabricate the notion of self. Detachment from the notion of self is detachment from a continuation of notions. Endurance of the absence of the notion of self is endurance of the absence of a continuation of notions.

### In stillness and in motion

Mindfulness, awareness, and endurance are the three essentials for cultivating detachment from the notion of self. Mindfulness is the first essential. Mindfulness is presence of mind. Mindfulness is cultivated in stillness and in motion. Mindfulness is cultivated in the absence of people and in the presence of people. Mindfulness is cultivated in favorable situations and in adverse situations.

Awareness is the second essential. Awareness is awareness of the presence of the notion of self. Awareness of the presence of the notion of self is cultivated in stillness and in motion. Awareness of the presence of the notion of self is cultivated in the absence of people and in the presence of people. Awareness of the presence of the notion of self is cultivated in favorable situations and in adverse situations.

Endurance is the third essential. Endurance is endurance of the absence of the notion of self. Endurance of the absence of the notion of self is cultivated in stillness and in motion. Endurance of the absence of the notion of self is cultivated in the absence of people and in the presence of people. Endurance of the absence of the notion of self is cultivated in favorable situations and in adverse situations.

### The emptiness of the self

The three essentials for cultivating detachment from the notion of self are mindfulness, awareness, and endurance. Mindfulness is presence of mind. Mindfulness is the foundation of the way. Awareness is awareness of the presence of the notion of self. Endurance is endurance of the absence of the notion of self.

To cultivate mindfulness, awareness, and endurance is to reveal the emptiness of the self. To cultivate mindfulness, awareness, and endurance is to reveal the true nature of the self. To cultivate mindfulness, awareness, and endurance is to cultivate the perfection of wisdom. To cultivate mindfulness, awareness, and endurance is to cease the affliction of ignorance.

# The emptiness of a person

### A person

The mind perceives the presence of entities. The mind perceives the presence of a person. A person is an entity. A person perceived by the mind is perceived to be endowed with inherent existence. To perceive a person to be endowed with inherent existence is to perceive a person to exist independently from everything else. To perceive a person to be endowed with inherent existence is to perceive a person as a separate and distinct entity. A person is a person endowed with inherent existence. A person and the inherent existence indwelling in a person are inseparable.

### The emptiness of a person

A person is empty. A person is devoid of inherent existence. The emptiness of a person is the absence of inherent existence a person is perceived to be endowed with. The emptiness of a person is the true nature of a person. The absence of inherent existence is the true nature of a person.

### The emptiness of a person

A person is empty. A person is devoid of inherent existence. A person is composed of the five skandhas. A person is a composition of the five skandhas. The five skandhas are form, feeling, thinking, volition, and consciousness. Form constitutes the body. Feeling, thinking, volition, and consciousness constitute the mind. A person is composed of the five skandhas. That which is composed of the five skandhas is dependent on the five skandhas. That which is dependent on the five skandhas cannot exist independently from the five skandhas. That which cannot exist independently from the five skandhas cannot exist independently from everything else. That which cannot exist independently from everything else cannot be endowed with inherent existence. That which cannot be endowed with inherent existence is devoid of inherent existence. That which is devoid of inherent existence is empty. A person is devoid of inherent existence. A person is empty. The emptiness of a person is the absence of inherent existence a person is perceived to be endowed with. That which is composed is inevitably empty. A person is composed of form, feeling, thinking, volition, and consciousness and therefore empty. To understand that a person can as a composition not be endowed with inherent existence is to understand the impossibility of a person to be endowed with inherent existence. To understand that a person can as a composition not be endowed with inherent existence is to understand conceptually the emptiness of a person.

### The fundamental absence of a person

A person is fundamentally absent. A person has never come into existence. That which is fundamentally absent is not. A person is not. A person is not a person. That which is fundamentally absent is inexpressible. A person is inexpressible. The fundamental absence of a person is the true nature of a person.

### The fundamental absence of a person

A person is empty. A person is devoid of inherent existence. The emptiness of a person is the absence of inherent existence a person is perceived to be endowed with. From the absence of inherent existence indwelling in a person follows the absence of a person. From the emptiness of a person follows the fundamental absence of a person. A person devoid of inherent existence is not a person. A person devoid of inherent existence is not. A person is fundamentally absent.

### The fundamental absence of a person

A person is fundamentally absent. A person is a composition of the five skandhas. The five skandhas are form, feeling, thinking, volition, and consciousness. Form, feeling, thinking, volition, and consciousness cannot constitute a person. Form, feeling, thinking, volition, and consciousness cannot constitute an entity. A person has never come into existence. A person is fundamentally absent. Compositions have never come into existence. Compositions are fundamentally absent. A person is not a person, because it is a composition. A person is a composition and therefore not a person. To understand conceptually the fundamental absence of a person is to understand conceptually the emptiness of a person.

### The notion of a person

The mind perceives the presence of a person. The perception of a person is caused by the presence of the notion of a person. The notion of a person arises from the mind. The mind is that which gives rise to the notion of a person. The notion of a person comes into being by way of thinking. Thinking is the coming together of the mind, the notion of a person, and the consciousness of the mind. The mind fabricates the notion of a person and it mistakes the presence of the notion of a person for a truly existent person. A person perceived by the mind is the notion of a person fabricated by the mind.

### The notion of inherent existence

The mind perceives the presence of a person. A person perceived by the mind is perceived to be endowed with inherent existence. The perception of inherent existence is caused by the presence of the notion of inherent existence. The notion of inherent existence arises from the mind. The mind is that which gives rise to the notion of inherent existence. The notion of inherent existence comes into being by way of thinking. Thinking is the coming together of the mind, the notion of inherent existence, and the consciousness of the mind. The mind fabricates the notion of inherent existence and it mistakes the presence of the notion of inherent existence for inherent existence. Inherent existence a person is perceived to be endowed with is the notion of inherent existence fabricated by the mind.

### An inherently existent person

The mind perceives an inherently existent person. An inherently existent person is a person endowed with inherent existence. The perception of an inherently existent person is caused by the presence of the notion of a person and the presence of the notion of inherent existence. The mind gives rise to the notion of a person and the notion of inherent existence and it mistakes the presence of the notion of a person and the presence of the notion of inherent existence for an inherently existent person.

### Perception

The mind perceives the presence of a person. A person, however, has never come into existence. A person is fundamentally absent. The mind perceives that which is fundamentally absent. The perception of a person is caused by the presence of the notion of a person. The mind gives rise to the notion of a person and it mistakes the presence of the notion of a person for a truly existent person. The presence of the notion of a person causes the perception of a person. The presence of the notion of a person causes the perception of that which is fundamentally absent. The mind perceives that which is fundamentally absent, because it fabricates a notion of that which is fundamentally absent.

A person is perceived to be endowed with inherent existence. A person, however, is devoid of inherent existence. All is devoid of inherent existence. Inherent existence is fundamentally absent. The mind perceives that which is devoid of inherent existence to be endowed with inherent existence. The perception of inherent existence is caused by

107

the presence of the notion of inherent existence. The mind gives rise to the notion of inherent existence and it mistakes the presence of the notion of inherent existence for inherent existence. The presence of the notion of inherent existence causes the perception of inherent existence. The mind perceives a person to be endowed with inherent existence, because it fabricates the notion of inherent existence. The mind perceives that which is devoid of inherent existence to be endowed with inherent existence, because it fabricates the notion of inherent existence.

### Revealing the fundamental absence of a person

A person is fundamentally absent. A person has never come into existence. The fundamental absence of a person is the true nature of a person. The fundamental absence of a person is revealed in the absence of the notion of a person. The perception of a person is caused by the presence of the notion of a person. The perception of a person does not come into being in the absence of the notion of a person. The absence of the notion of a person is the absence of the perception of a person. The absence of the perception of a person reveals the fundamental absence of a person. The fundamental absence of a person is revealed in the absence of the notion of a person.

### Revealing the emptiness of a person

A person is empty. A person is devoid of inherent existence. The emptiness of a person is the absence of inherent existence a person is perceived to be endowed with. The emptiness of a person is revealed in the absence of the notion of inherent existence. The perception of inherent existence is caused by the presence of the notion of inherent existence. The perception of inherent existence does not come into being in the absence of the notion of inherent existence. The absence of the notion of inherent existence is the absence of the perception of inherent existence. The absence of the perception of inherent existence reveals the emptiness of a person. The emptiness of a person is revealed in the absence of the notion of inherent existence.

### Revealing the true nature of a person

A person is empty and fundamentally absent. The emptiness and fundamental absence of a person are the true nature of a person. The emptiness and fundamental absence of a person are revealed in the absence of the notion of a person and the absence of the notion of inherent existence. The perception of an inherently existent person is caused by the presence of the notion of a person and the presence of the notion of inherent existence. The perception of an inherently existent person does not come into being in the absence of the notion of a person and the absence of the notion of inherent existence. The absence of the notion of a person and the absence of the notion of inherent existence are the absence of a person perceived to exist inherently and the absence of inherent existence a person is perceived to be endowed with. The absence of inherent existence a person is perceived to be endowed with is the emptiness of a person. The emptiness and fundamental absence of a person are revealed in the absence of the notion of a person and the absence of the notion of inherent existence.

### Detachment from the notion of a person

A person is empty and fundamentally absent. The emptiness and fundamental absence of a person are the true nature of a person. The emptiness and fundamental absence of a person are revealed in the absence of the notion of a person and the absence of the notion of inherent existence. The absence of the notion of a person and the absence of the notion of inherent existence are arrived at by detaching from the notion of a person. To detach from the notion of a person is to not entertain the notion of a person. To detach from the notion of a person is to discontinue the formation of the notion of a person. To detach from the notion of a person is to seek the immediate absence of the notion of a person.

To detach from the notion of a person is to withstand the fierceness of the arising of the notion of a person. To detach from the notion of a person is to endure patiently the absence of the notion of a person.

### Detachment from the notion of inherent existence

A person is empty and fundamentally absent. The emptiness and fundamental absence of a person are the true nature of a person. The emptiness and fundamental absence of a person are revealed in the absence of the notion of a person and the absence of the notion of inherent existence. The absence of the notion of a person and the absence of the notion of inherent existence are arrived at by detaching from the notion of inherent existence. To detach from the notion of inherent existence is to not entertain the notion of inherent existence. To detach from the notion of inherent existence is to discontinue the formation of the notion of inherent existence. To detach from the notion of inherent existence is to seek the immediate absence of the notion of inherent existence. To detach from the notion of inherent existence is to withstand the fierceness of the arising of the notion of inherent existence. To detach from the notion of inherent existence is to endure patiently the absence of the notion of inherent existence.

### The perfection of wisdom

The perfection of wisdom is the cultivation of wisdom. Wisdom is understanding the true nature of all. Wisdom is understanding the true nature of a person. The emptiness and fundamental absence of a person are the true nature of a person. The emptiness and fundamental absence of a person are revealed by cultivating detachment from the notion of a person. Wisdom is revealed by cultivating detachment from the notion of a person. To cultivate detachment from the notion of a person is to cultivate the perfection of wisdom. To endure patiently the absence of the notion of a person is to cultivate the perfection of wisdom.

# Detachment from the notion of a person

### The three essentials

Detachment is the way. Detachment is detachment from notions of entities. Detachment is detachment from the notion of a person. The three essentials for cultivating detachment from the notion of a person are mindfulness, awareness, and endurance. Mindfulness is presence of mind. Awareness is awareness of the presence of the notion of a person. Endurance is endurance of the absence of the notion of a person.

### Mindfulness

Mindfulness is the first essential. Mindfulness is presence of mind. To be mindful is to be mindful of the presence of a sense object. To be mindful is to be mindful of form, sound, touch, or notions. Mindfulness is the foundation of the way. The absence of mindfulness is the absence of the way.

### Awareness

Awareness is the second essential. Awareness is awareness of the presence of the notion of a person. A person perceived by the mind is the notion of a person fabricated by the mind. To be aware of the notion of a person is to be aware of that which causes the perception of a person. To be aware of the notion of a person is to be aware of that the mind seeks to detach from.

The notion of a person arises from the mind. It comes into being by way of thinking. The mind that seeks awareness of the notion of a person must seek within itself. The mind must reflect back. To cultivate awareness is to reflect back and to discern the presence of the notion of a person. To cultivate awareness is to reflect back and to mindfully observe the presence of the notion of a person.

### Awareness

The mind that is dwelling on the notion of a person is not aware of
its dwelling. The mind that is not aware of its dwelling cannot detach
from the notion of a person.

The mind that is dwelling on the notion of a person must reflect back
and be aware of its dwelling. The mind can detach from the notion of a
person only if it is aware of its dwelling.

### Endurance

Endurance is the third essential. Endurance is patient endurance of
the absence of the notion of a person. The notion of a person forms
and ceases from moment to moment. A notion of a person that was is
followed by a notion of a person that is. A notion of a person that is is
followed by a notion of a person that will be. The notion of a person
is a succession of notions. The notion of a person is a continuation of
notions. Each notion of a person insists on its arising. Each notion of
a person arises fiercely. The fierceness of the arising of the notion of a
person is the mind's compulsion to fabricate the notion of a person. To
endure patiently the absence of the notion of a person is to withstand
from moment to moment the fierceness of the arising of the notion of
a person. To endure patiently the absence of the notion of a person is
to oppose from moment to moment the mind's compulsion to fabricate
the notion of a person. Detachment from the notion of a person is
detachment from a continuation of notions. Endurance of the absence
of the notion of a person is endurance of the absence of a continuation
of notions.

### In stillness and in motion

Mindfulness, awareness, and endurance are the three essentials for cultivating detachment from the notion of a person. Mindfulness is the first essential. Mindfulness is presence of mind. Mindfulness is cultivated in stillness and in motion. Mindfulness is cultivated in the absence of people and in the presence of people. Mindfulness is cultivated in favorable situations and in adverse situations.

Awareness is the second essential. Awareness is awareness of the presence of the notion of a person. Awareness of the presence of the notion of a person is cultivated in stillness and in motion. Awareness of the presence of the notion of a person is cultivated in the absence of people and in the presence of people. Awareness of the presence of the notion of a person is cultivated in favorable situations and in adverse situations.

Endurance is the third essential. Endurance is endurance of the absence of the notion of a person. Endurance of the absence of the notion of a person is cultivated in stillness and in motion. Endurance of the absence of the notion of a person is cultivated in the absence of people and in the presence of people. Endurance of the absence of the notion of a person is cultivated in favorable situations and in adverse situations.


### The emptiness of a person

The three essentials for cultivating detachment from the notion of a person are mindfulness, awareness, and endurance. Mindfulness is presence of mind. Mindfulness is the foundation of the way. Awareness is awareness of the presence of the notion of a person. Endurance is endurance of the absence of the notion of a person.

To cultivate mindfulness, awareness, and endurance is to reveal the emptiness of a person. To cultivate mindfulness, awareness, and endurance is to reveal the true nature of a person. To cultivate mindfulness, awareness, and endurance is to cultivate the perfection of wisdom. To cultivate mindfulness, awareness, and endurance is to cease the affliction of ignorance.

# Detachment from the notion of a person

### Form is devoid of a person

The mind perceives the presence of a person in the dust of form. Form is that which is perceived by the eyes. The eyes come together with form and the mind gives rise to the notion of a person. The coming together of the eyes, form, and the consciousness of the eyes conditions the coming together of the mind, the notion of a person, and the consciousness of the mind. Seeing conditions thinking. The notion of a person arises in the presence of form. The presence of the notion of a person causes the perception of a truly existent person.

The mind falsely believes that form perceived by the eyes and the notion of a person fabricated by the mind are one and the same. The mind perceives the presence of a person in the dust of form. A person, however, has never existed in the dust of form. Form is devoid of entities. Form is devoid of a person. A person has never come into existence. A person is fundamentally absent. That which is perceived by the eyes is ungraspable and inexpressible. Form is ungraspable and inexpressible.

The fundamental absence of a person is revealed in the absence of the notion of a person. The perception of a person is caused by the presence of the notion of a person. The perception of a person does not come into being in the absence of the notion of a person. The absence of the notion of a person is the absence of the perception of a person. The absence of the notion of a person is arrived at by detaching from the notion of a person.

To detach from the notion of a person is to discontinue the formation of the notion of a person while the eyes are perceiving form. To detach from the notion of a person is to cease the coming together of the mind, the notion of a person, and the consciousness of the mind conditioned by the coming together of the eyes, form, and the consciousness of the eyes. To detach from the notion of a person arising in the presence of form is to reveal that form is devoid of a person.

### Sound is devoid of a person

The mind perceives the presence of a person in the dust of sound. Sound is that which is perceived by the ears. The ears come together with sound and the mind gives rise to the notion of a person. The coming together of the ears, sound, and the consciousness of the ears conditions the coming together of the mind, the notion of a person, and the consciousness of the mind. Hearing conditions thinking. The notion of a person arises in the presence of sound. The presence of the notion of a person causes the perception of a truly existent person.

The mind falsely believes that sound perceived by the ears and the notion of a person fabricated by the mind are one and the same. The mind perceives the presence of a person in the dust of sound. A person, however, has never existed in the dust of sound. Sound is devoid of entities. Sound is devoid of a person. A person has never come into existence. A person is fundamentally absent. That which is perceived by the ears is ungraspable and inexpressible. Sound is ungraspable and inexpressible.

The fundamental absence of a person is revealed in the absence of the notion of a person. The perception of a person is caused by the presence of the notion of a person. The perception of a person does not come into being in the absence of the notion of a person. The absence of the notion of a person is the absence of the perception of a person. The absence of the notion of a person is arrived at by detaching from the notion of a person.

To detach from the notion of a person is to discontinue the formation of the notion of a person while the ears are perceiving sound. To detach from the notion of a person is to cease the coming together of the mind, the notion of a person, and the consciousness of the mind conditioned by the coming together of the ears, sound, and the consciousness of the ears. To detach from the notion of a person arising in the presence of sound is to reveal that sound is devoid of a person.

# The emptiness of the body

### The body

The mind perceives the presence of entities. The mind perceives the presence of a body. The body is an entity. The body perceived by the mind is perceived to be endowed with inherent existence. To perceive the body to be endowed with inherent existence is to perceive the body to exist independently from everything else. To perceive the body to be endowed with inherent existence is to perceive the body as a separate and distinct entity. The body is a body endowed with inherent existence. The body and the inherent existence indwelling in the body are inseparable.

### The emptiness of the body

The body is empty. The body is devoid of inherent existence. The emptiness of the body is the absence of inherent existence the body is perceived to be endowed with. The emptiness of the body is the true nature of the body. The absence of inherent existence is the true nature of the body.

### The fundamental absence of the body

The body is fundamentally absent. A body has never come into existence. That which is fundamentally absent is not. The body is not. The body is not a body. That which is fundamentally absent is inexpressible. The body is inexpressible. The fundamental absence of the body is the true nature of the body.

**The fundamental absence of the body**

The body is empty. The body is devoid of inherent existence. The emptiness of the body is the absence of inherent existence the body is perceived to be endowed with. From the absence of inherent existence indwelling in the body follows the absence of the body. From the emptiness of the body follows the fundamental absence of the body. A body devoid of inherent existence is not a body. A body devoid of inherent existence is not. The body is fundamentally absent.

**A composition of entities**

The body pertains to and arises from form. Form is the first skandha. The five skandhas are form, feeling, thinking, volition, and consciousness. Form is matter. Entities pertaining to matter are composed of smaller entities. Entities pertaining to matter are compositions. The body is an entity composed of smaller entities. The body is a composition of smaller entities.

**The emptiness of the body (i)**

The body is empty. The body is a composition of a head, a torso, arms, hands, legs, and feet. That which is composed of a head, a torso, and limbs is dependent on a head, a torso, and limbs. That which is dependent on a head, a torso, and limbs cannot exist independently from a head, a torso, and limbs. That which cannot exist independently from a head, a torso, and limbs cannot exist independently from everything else. That which cannot exist independently from everything else cannot be endowed with inherent existence. That which cannot be endowed with inherent existence is devoid of inherent existence. That which is devoid of inherent existence is empty. The body is devoid of inherent existence. The body is empty. The emptiness of the body is the absence of inherent existence the body is perceived to be endowed with. That which is composed is inevitably empty. The body is composed of a head, a torso, arms, hands, legs, and feet and therefore empty. To

117

understand that the body can as a composition not be endowed with inherent existence is to understand the impossibility of the body to be endowed with inherent existence. To understand that the body can as a composition not be endowed with inherent existence is to understand conceptually the emptiness of the body.

### The fundamental absence of the body (i)

The body is fundamentally absent. The body is a composition of a head, a torso, and limbs. A head, a torso, and limbs cannot constitute a body. A head, a torso, and limbs cannot constitute a composition. A head can only constitute a head. A head can only constitute itself. A torso can only constitute a torso. A torso can only constitute itself. A limb can only constitute a limb. A limb can only constitute itself. A head, a torso, and limbs do not come together and declare to constitute a body. They do not come together and declare to constitute an entity. A body has never come into existence. The body is fundamentally absent. Compositions have never come into existence. Compositions are fundamentally absent. The body is not a body, because it is a composition. The body is a composition and therefore not a body. To understand conceptually the fundamental absence of the body is to understand conceptually the emptiness of the body.

### The emptiness of the body (ii)

The body is empty. The body is a composition of solids, liquids, and gases. That which is composed of solids, liquids, and gases is dependent on solids, liquids, and gases. That which is dependent on solids, liquids, and gases cannot exist independently from solids, liquids, and gases. That which cannot exist independently from solids, liquids, and gases cannot exist independently from everything else. That which cannot exist independently from everything else cannot be endowed with inherent existence. That which cannot be endowed with inherent existence is devoid of inherent existence. That which is devoid of inherent

118

existence is empty. The body is devoid of inherent existence. The body is empty. The emptiness of the body is the absence of inherent existence the body is perceived to be endowed with. That which is composed is inevitably empty. The body is composed of solids, liquids, and gases and therefore empty. To understand that the body can as a composition not be endowed with inherent existence is to understand the impossibility of the body to be endowed with inherent existence. To understand that the body can as a composition not be endowed with inherent existence is to understand conceptually the emptiness of the body.

### The fundamental absence of the body (ii)

The body is fundamentally absent. The body is a composition of solids, liquids, and gases. Solids, liquids, and gases cannot constitute a body. Solids, liquids, and gases cannot constitute a composition. A solid can only constitute a solid. A solid can only constitute itself. A liquid can only constitute a liquid. A liquid can only constitute itself. A gas can only constitute a gas. A gas can only constitute itself. Solids, liquids, and gases do not come together and declare to constitute a body. They do not come together and declare to constitute an entity. A body has never come into existence. The body is fundamentally absent. Compositions have never come into existence. Compositions are fundamentally absent. The body is not a body, because it is a composition. The body is a composition and therefore not a body. To understand conceptually the fundamental absence of the body is to understand conceptually the emptiness of the body.

### The emptiness of the body (iii)

The body is empty. The body is a composition of dust particles. That which is composed of dust particles is dependent on dust particles. That which is dependent on dust particles cannot exist independently from dust particles. That which cannot exist independently from dust particles cannot exist independently from everything else. That which cannot exist independently from everything else cannot be endowed with inherent existence. That which cannot be endowed with inherent existence is devoid of inherent existence. That which is devoid of inherent existence is empty. The body is devoid of inherent existence. The body is empty. The emptiness of the body is the absence of inherent existence the body is perceived to be endowed with. That which is composed is inevitably empty. The body is composed of dust particles and therefore empty. To understand that the body can as a composition not be endowed with inherent existence is to understand the impossibility of the body to be endowed with inherent existence. To understand that the body can as a composition not be endowed with inherent existence is to understand conceptually the emptiness of the body.

### The fundamental absence of the body (iii)

The body is fundamentally absent. The body is a composition of dust particles. Dust particles cannot constitute a body. Dust particles cannot constitute a composition. A dust particle can only constitute a dust particle. A dust particle can only constitute itself. A dust particle and another dust particle and yet other myriads of dust particles do not come together and declare to constitute a body. They do not come together and declare to constitute an entity. A body has never come into existence. The body is fundamentally absent. Compositions have never come into existence. Compositions are fundamentally absent. The body is not a body, because it is a composition. The body is a composition and therefore not a body. To understand conceptually the fundamental absence of the body is to understand conceptually the emptiness of the body.

### The notion of a body

The mind perceives the presence of a body. The perception of a body is caused by the presence of the notion of a body. The notion of a body arises from the mind. The mind is that which gives rise to the notion of a body. The notion of a body comes into being by way of thinking. Thinking is the coming together of the mind, the notion of a body, and the consciousness of the mind. The mind fabricates the notion of a body and it mistakes the presence of the notion of a body for a truly existent body. The body perceived by the mind is the notion of a body fabricated by the mind.

### The notion of inherent existence

The mind perceives the presence of a body. The body perceived by the mind is perceived to be endowed with inherent existence. The perception of inherent existence is caused by the presence of the notion of inherent existence. The notion of inherent existence arises from the mind. The mind is that which gives rise to the notion of inherent existence. The notion of inherent existence comes into being by way of thinking. Thinking is the coming together of the mind, the notion of inherent existence, and the consciousness of the mind. The mind fabricates the notion of inherent existence and it mistakes the presence of the notion of inherent existence for inherent existence. Inherent existence the body is perceived to be endowed with is the notion of inherent existence fabricated by the mind.

### An inherently existent body

The mind perceives an inherently existent body. An inherently existent body is a body endowed with inherent existence. The perception of an inherently existent body is caused by the presence of the notion of a body and the presence of the notion of inherent existence. The mind gives rise to the notion of a body and the notion of inherent existence and it mistakes the presence of the notion of a body and the presence of the notion of inherent existence for an inherently existent body.

## Perception

The mind perceives the presence of a body. A body, however, has never come into existence. The body is fundamentally absent. The mind perceives that which is fundamentally absent. The perception of a body is caused by the presence of the notion of a body. The mind gives rise to the notion of a body and it mistakes the presence of the notion of a body for a truly existent body. The presence of the notion of a body causes the perception of a body. The presence of the notion of a body causes the perception of that which is fundamentally absent. The mind perceives that which is fundamentally absent, because it fabricates a notion of that which is fundamentally absent.

The body is perceived to be endowed with inherent existence. The body, however, is devoid of inherent existence. All is devoid of inherent existence. Inherent existence is fundamentally absent. The mind perceives that which is devoid of inherent existence to be endowed with inherent existence. The perception of inherent existence is caused by the presence of the notion of inherent existence. The mind gives rise to the notion of inherent existence and it mistakes the presence of the notion of inherent existence for inherent existence. The presence of the notion of inherent existence causes the perception of inherent existence. The mind perceives the body to be endowed with inherent existence, because it fabricates the notion of inherent existence. The mind perceives that which is devoid of inherent existence to be endowed with inherent existence, because it fabricates the notion of inherent existence.

### Revealing the fundamental absence of the body

The body is fundamentally absent. A body has never come into existence. The fundamental absence of the body is the true nature of the body. The fundamental absence of the body is revealed in the absence of the notion of a body. The perception of a body is caused by the presence of the notion of a body. The perception of a body does not come into being in the absence of the notion of a body. The absence of the notion of a body is the absence of the perception of a body. The absence of the perception of a body reveals the fundamental absence of the body. The fundamental absence of the body is revealed in the absence of the notion of a body.

### Revealing the emptiness of the body

The body is empty. The body is devoid of inherent existence. The emptiness of the body is the absence of inherent existence the body is perceived to be endowed with. The emptiness of the body is revealed in the absence of the notion of inherent existence. The perception of inherent existence is caused by the presence of the notion of inherent existence. The perception of inherent existence does not come into being in the absence of the notion of inherent existence. The absence of the notion of inherent existence is the absence of the perception of inherent existence. The absence of the perception of inherent existence reveals the emptiness of the body. The emptiness of the body is revealed in the absence of the notion of inherent existence.

### Revealing the true nature of the body

The body is empty and fundamentally absent. The emptiness and fundamental absence of the body are the true nature of the body. The emptiness and fundamental absence of the body are revealed in the absence of the notion of a body and the absence of the notion of inherent existence. The perception of an inherently existent body is caused by the presence of the notion of a body and the presence of the notion of inherent existence. The perception of an inherently existent body does not come into being in the absence of the notion of a body and the absence of the notion of inherent existence. The absence of the notion of a body and the absence of the notion of inherent existence are the absence of a body perceived to exist inherently and the absence of inherent existence the body is perceived to be endowed with. The absence of inherent existence the body is perceived to be endowed with is the emptiness of the body. The emptiness and fundamental absence of the body are revealed in the absence of the notion of a body and the absence of the notion of inherent existence.


### Detachment from the notion of a body

The body is empty and fundamentally absent. The emptiness and fundamental absence of the body are the true nature of the body. The emptiness and fundamental absence of the body are revealed in the absence of the notion of a body and the absence of the notion of inherent existence. The absence of the notion of a body and the absence of the notion of inherent existence are arrived at by detaching from the notion of a body. To detach from the notion of a body is to not entertain the notion of a body. To detach from the notion of a body is to discontinue the formation of the notion of a body. To detach from the notion of a body is to seek the immediate absence of the notion of a body. To detach from the notion of a body is to withstand the fierceness of the arising of the notion of a body. To detach from the notion of a body is to endure patiently the absence of the notion of a body.

**Detachment from the notion of inherent existence**

The body is empty and fundamentally absent. The emptiness and fundamental absence of the body are the true nature of the body. The emptiness and fundamental absence of the body are revealed in the absence of the notion of a body and the absence of the notion of inherent existence. The absence of the notion of a body and the absence of the notion of inherent existence are arrived at by detaching from the notion of inherent existence. To detach from the notion of inherent existence is to not entertain the notion of inherent existence. To detach from the notion of inherent existence is to discontinue the formation of the notion of inherent existence. To detach from the notion of inherent existence is to seek the immediate absence of the notion of inherent existence. To detach from the notion of inherent existence is to withstand the fierceness of the arising of the notion of inherent existence. To detach from the notion of inherent existence is to endure patiently the absence of the notion of inherent existence.

**The perfection of wisdom**

The perfection of wisdom is the cultivation of wisdom. Wisdom is understanding the true nature of all. Wisdom is understanding the true nature of the body. The emptiness and fundamental absence of the body are the true nature of the body. The emptiness and fundamental absence of the body are revealed by cultivating detachment from the notion of a body. Wisdom is revealed by cultivating detachment from the notion of a body. To cultivate detachment from the notion of a body is to cultivate the perfection of wisdom. To endure patiently the absence of the notion of a body is to cultivate the perfection of wisdom.

# Detachment from the notion of a body

### The three essentials

Detachment is the way. Detachment is detachment from notions of entities. Detachment is detachment from the notion of a body. The three essentials for cultivating detachment from the notion of a body are mindfulness, awareness, and endurance. Mindfulness is presence of mind. Awareness is awareness of the presence of the notion of a body. Endurance is endurance of the absence of the notion of a body.

### Mindfulness

Mindfulness is the first essential. Mindfulness is presence of mind. To be mindful is to be mindful of the presence of a sense object. To be mindful is to be mindful of form, sound, touch, or notions. Mindfulness is the foundation of the way. The absence of mindfulness is the absence of the way.

### Awareness

Awareness is the second essential. Awareness is awareness of the presence of the notion of a body. The body perceived by the mind is the notion of a body fabricated by the mind. To be aware of the notion of a body is to be aware of that which causes the perception of a body. To be aware of the notion of a body is to be aware of that the mind seeks to detach from.

The notion of a body arises from the mind. It comes into being by way of thinking. The mind that seeks awareness of the notion of a body must seek within itself. The mind must reflect back. To cultivate awareness is to reflect back and to discern the presence of the notion of a body. To cultivate awareness is to reflect back and to mindfully observe the presence of the notion of a body.

## Awareness

The mind that is dwelling on the notion of a body is not aware of its dwelling. The mind that is not aware of its dwelling cannot detach from the notion of a body.

The mind that is dwelling on the notion of a body must reflect back and be aware of its dwelling. The mind can detach from the notion of a body only if it is aware of its dwelling.

## Endurance

Endurance is the third essential. Endurance is patient endurance of the absence of the notion of a body. The notion of a body forms and ceases from moment to moment. A notion of a body that was is followed by a notion of a body that is. A notion of a body that is is followed by a notion of a body that will be. The notion of a body is a succession of notions. The notion of a body is a continuation of notions. Each notion of a body insists on its arising. Each notion of a body arises fiercely. The fierceness of the arising of the notion of a body is the mind's incessant compulsion to fabricate the notion of a body. To endure patiently the absence of the notion of a body is to withstand from moment to moment the fierceness of the arising of the notion of a body. To endure patiently the absence of the notion of a body is to oppose from moment to moment the mind's compulsion to fabricate the notion of a body. Detachment from the notion of a body is detachment from a continuation of notions. Endurance of the absence of the notion of a body is endurance of the absence of a continuation of notions.

### In stillness and in motion

Mindfulness, awareness, and endurance are the three essentials for cultivating detachment from the notion of a body. Mindfulness is the first essential. Mindfulness is presence of mind. Mindfulness is cultivated in stillness and in motion. Mindfulness is cultivated in the absence of people and in the presence of people. Mindfulness is cultivated in favorable situations and in adverse situations.

Awareness is the second essential. Awareness is awareness of the presence of the notion of a body. Awareness of the presence of the notion of a body is cultivated in stillness and in motion. Awareness of the presence of the notion of a body is cultivated in the absence of people and in the presence of people. Awareness of the presence of the notion of a body is cultivated in favorable situations and in adverse situations.

Endurance is the third essential. Endurance is endurance of the absence of the notion of a body. Endurance of the absence of the notion of a body is cultivated in stillness and in motion. Endurance of the absence of the notion of a body is cultivated in the absence of people and in the presence of people. Endurance of the absence of the notion of a body is cultivated in favorable situations and in adverse situations.


### The emptiness of the body

The three essentials for cultivating detachment from the notion of a body are mindfulness, awareness, and endurance. Mindfulness is presence of mind. Mindfulness is the foundation of the way. Awareness is awareness of the presence of the notion of a body. Endurance is endurance of the absence of the notion of a body.

To cultivate mindfulness, awareness, and endurance is to reveal the emptiness of the body. To cultivate mindfulness, awareness, and endurance is to reveal the true nature of the body. To cultivate mindfulness, awareness, and endurance is to cultivate the perfection of wisdom. To cultivate mindfulness, awareness, and endurance is to cease the affliction of ignorance.

# Detachment from the notion of a body

## Form is devoid of a body

The mind perceives the presence of a body in the dust of form. Form is that which is perceived by the eyes. The eyes come together with form and the mind gives rise to the notion of a body. The coming together of the eyes, form, and the consciousness of the eyes conditions the coming together of the mind, the notion of a body, and the consciousness of the mind. Seeing conditions thinking. The notion of a body arises in the presence of form. The presence of the notion of a body causes the perception of a truly existent body.

The mind falsely believes that form perceived by the eyes and the notion of a body fabricated by the mind are one and the same. The mind perceives the presence of a body in the dust of form. A body, however, has never existed in the dust of form. Form is devoid of entities. Form is devoid of a body. A body has never come into existence. The body is fundamentally absent. That which is perceived by the eyes is ungraspable and inexpressible. Form is ungraspable and inexpressible.

The fundamental absence of the body is revealed in the absence of the notion of a body. The perception of a body is caused by the presence of the notion of a body. The perception of a body does not come into being in the absence of the notion of a body. The absence of the notion of a body is the absence of the perception of a body. The absence of the notion of a body is arrived at by detaching from the notion of a body.

To detach from the notion of a body is to discontinue the formation of the notion of a body while the eyes are perceiving form. To detach from the notion of a body is to cease the coming together of the mind, the notion of a body, and the consciousness of the mind conditioned by the coming together of the eyes, form, and the consciousness of the eyes. To detach from the notion of a body arising in the presence of form is to reveal that form is devoid of a body.

# The emptiness of a sentient being

## The emptiness of a sentient being

The mind perceives the presence of entities. The mind perceives the presence of sentient beings. A sentient being is an entity. The six classes of sentient beings are hell beings, hungry ghosts, animals, human beings, asuras, and heavenly beings. A sentient being perceived by the mind is perceived to be endowed with inherent existence. To perceive a sentient being to be endowed with inherent existence is to perceive a sentient being to exist independently from everything else. To perceive a sentient being to be endowed with inherent existence is to perceive a sentient being as a separate and distinct entity. A sentient being is a sentient being endowed with inherent existence. A sentient being and the inherent existence indwelling in a sentient being are inseparable.

A sentient being is devoid of inherent existence. A sentient being is composed of the five skandhas. The five skandhas are form, feeling, thinking, volition, and consciousness. That which is composed of form, feeling, thinking, volition, and consciousness is dependent on form, feeling, thinking, volition, and consciousness. That which is dependent on form, feeling, thinking, volition, and consciousness cannot exist independently from form, feeling, thinking, volition, and consciousness. That which cannot exist independently from form, feeling, thinking, volition, and consciousness cannot exist independently from everything else. That which cannot exist independently from everything else is devoid of inherent existence. A sentient being is devoid of inherent existence.

A sentient being is fundamentally absent. A sentient being is composed of the five skandhas. The five skandhas are form, feeling, thinking, volition, and consciousness. Form, feeling, thinking, volition, and consciousness cannot constitute a sentient being. Form, feeling, thinking, volition, and consciousness cannot constitute an entity. A sentient being has never come into existence. A sentient being is fundamentally absent. A composition of form, feeling, thinking, volition, and consciousness has never come into existence. A composition of form, feeling, thinking, volition, and consciousness is fundamentally absent. A sentient being is not a sentient being, because it is a composition. A sentient being is a composition and therefore not a sentient being.

All is empty. All is devoid of inherent existence. A sentient being is empty. A sentient being is devoid of inherent existence. The emptiness of a sentient being is the absence of inherent existence a sentient being is perceived to be endowed with. From the emptiness of a sentient being follows the fundamental absence of a sentient being. A sentient being is fundamentally absent. Such an entity has never come into existence. That which is fundamentally absent is not. A sentient being is not. A sentient being is not a sentient being. That which is fundamentally absent is inexpressible. A sentient being is inexpressible. The emptiness and fundamental absence of a sentient being are the true nature of a sentient being.

A sentient being perceived by the mind is the notion of a sentient being fabricated by the mind. Inherent existence a sentient being is perceived to be endowed with is the notion of inherent existence fabricated by the mind. The presence of the notion of a sentient being and the presence of the notion of inherent existence cause the perception of an inherently existent sentient being. It is by way of the notion of inherent existence that a sentient being is perceived to exist independently from everything else. It is by way of the notion of inherent existence that a sentient being is perceived as a separate and distinct entity. The fierceness of the arising of the notion of a sentient being is the mind's compulsion to fabricate the notion of a sentient being.

A sentient being is empty and fundamentally absent. The emptiness and fundamental absence of a sentient being are revealed in the absence of the notion of a sentient being and the absence of the notion of inherent existence. The absence of the notion of a sentient being and the absence of the notion of inherent existence are the absence of a sentient being perceived to exist inherently and the absence of inherent existence a sentient being is perceived to be endowed with. The absence of inherent existence a sentient being is perceived to be endowed with is the emptiness of a sentient being. The absence of the notion of a sentient

131

being and the absence of the notion of inherent existence are arrived at by detaching from the notion of a sentient being.

To detach from the notion of a sentient being is to not entertain the notion of a sentient being. To detach from the notion of a sentient being is to discontinue the formation of the notion of a sentient being. To detach from the notion of a sentient being is to seek the immediate absence of the notion of a sentient being. To detach from the notion of a sentient being is to withstand the fierceness of the arising of the notion of a sentient being. To detach from the notion of a sentient being is to endure patiently the absence of the notion of a sentient being. To detach from the notion of a sentient being is to reveal the emptiness and fundamental absence of a sentient being.

### The emptiness of a bodhisattva

The mind perceives the presence of entities. The mind perceives the presence of a bodhisattva. A bodhisattva is an entity. A bodhisattva is a sentient being that enlightens all sentient beings. 'Bodhi' is Sanskrit and means 'awakening' or 'enlightenment'. 'Sattva' is Sanskrit and means 'sentient being'. A bodhisattva perceived by the mind is perceived to be endowed with inherent existence. To perceive a bodhisattva to be endowed with inherent existence is to perceive a bodhisattva to exist independently from everything else. To perceive a bodhisattva to be endowed with inherent existence is to perceive a bodhisattva as a separate and distinct entity. A bodhisattva is a bodhisattva endowed with inherent existence. A bodhisattva and the inherent existence indwelling in a bodhisattva are inseparable.

All is empty. All is devoid of inherent existence. A bodhisattva is empty. A bodhisattva is devoid of inherent existence. The emptiness of a bodhisattva is the absence of inherent existence a bodhisattva is perceived to be endowed with. From the emptiness of a bodhisattva follows the fundamental absence of a bodhisattva. A bodhisattva is fundamentally absent. A bodhisattva has never come into existence. That which is fundamentally absent is not. A bodhisattva is not. A bodhisattva is not a bodhisattva. That which is fundamentally absent is inexpressible. A bodhisattva is inexpressible. The emptiness and fundamental absence of a bodhisattva are the true nature of a bodhisattva.

A bodhisattva perceived by the mind is the notion of a bodhisattva fabricated by the mind. Inherent existence a bodhisattva is perceived to be endowed with is the notion of inherent existence fabricated by the mind. The presence of the notion of a bodhisattva and the presence of the notion of inherent existence cause the perception of an inherently existent bodhisattva. It is by way of the notion of inherent existence that a bodhisattva is perceived to exist independently from everything else. It is by way of the notion of inherent existence that a bodhisattva is perceived as a separate and distinct entity. The fierceness of the arising of the notion of a bodhisattva is the mind's compulsion to fabricate the notion of a bodhisattva.

A bodhisattva is empty and fundamentally absent. The emptiness and fundamental absence of a bodhisattva are revealed in the absence of the notion of a bodhisattva and the absence of the notion of inherent existence. The absence of the notion of a bodhisattva and the absence of the notion of inherent existence are the absence of a bodhisattva perceived to exist inherently and the absence of inherent existence a bodhisattva is perceived to be endowed with. The absence of inherent existence a bodhisattva is perceived to be endowed with is the emptiness of a bodhisattva. The absence of the notion of a bodhisattva and the absence of the notion of inherent existence are arrived at by detaching from the notion of inherent existence.

To detach from the notion of inherent existence is to not entertain the notion of inherent existence. To detach from the notion of inherent existence is to cease the formation of the notion of inherent existence. To detach from the notion of inherent existence is to seek the immediate absence of the notion of inherent existence. To detach from the notion of inherent existence is to withstand the fierceness of the arising of the notion of inherent existence. To detach from the notion of inherent existence is to endure patiently the absence of the notion of inherent existence. To detach from the notion of inherent existence is to reveal the emptiness and fundamental absence of a bodhisattva.

The Diamond Sutra says, "Subhuti, a bodhisattva who realizes that all is devoid of a self and that all is devoid of inherent existence is, the Tathagata says, a true bodhisattva."

# Contemplation

### Elephants

Contemplating the emptiness of entities is important. The emptiness of entities can be contemplated by contemplating the emptiness of compositions. Contemplating the emptiness of entities gives rise to a conceptual understanding of emptiness. Contemplation is the cause. Understanding is the effect. To contemplate the emptiness of entities is to contemplate it a thousand times, ten thousand times, and a hundred thousand times. The mind must contemplate the emptiness of entities over and over until there is no doubt that all that is being perceived is empty and fundamentally absent. The mind must settle this once and for all until there is not a single moment of doubt and not a single moment of hesitation. If there is doubt and hesitation, there will be doubt and hesitation, when the mind is plagued by desire and hatred. If there is doubt and hesitation, there will be doubt and hesitation, when the mind is shrouded in pleasure and suffering. Understanding the emptiness of entities conceptually must be like elephants trampling on grass. When elephants trample on grass, the grass bends down and it does not rise up again. When the mind contemplates emptiness, all doubts must vanish at once and not arise again. Contemplating emptiness is important.

### Compositions

A forest is empty. A forest is devoid of inherent existence. The emptiness of a forest can be contemplated by contemplating the emptiness of a forest as a composition of trees.

A mountain is empty. A mountain is devoid of inherent existence. The emptiness of a mountain can be contemplated by contemplating the emptiness of a mountain as a composition of rocks.

A river is empty. A river is devoid of inherent existence. The emptiness of a river can be contemplated by contemplating the emptiness of a river as a composition of masses of water.

A tree is empty. A tree is devoid of inherent existence. The emptiness of a tree can be contemplated by contemplating the emptiness of a tree as a composition of roots, a trunk, branches, and leaves.

A garden is empty. A garden is devoid of inherent existence. The emptiness of a garden can be contemplated by contemplating the emptiness of a garden as a composition of flowers, trees, and ponds.

A world is empty. A world is devoid of inherent existence. The emptiness of a world can be contemplated by contemplating the emptiness of a world as a composition of dust particles.

### Compositions

The self is empty. The self is devoid of inherent existence. The emptiness of the self can be contemplated by contemplating the emptiness of the self as a composition of the five skandhas.

A person is empty. A person is devoid of inherent existence. The emptiness of a person can be contemplated by contemplating the emptiness of a person as a composition of the five skandhas.

The body is empty. The body is devoid of inherent existence. The emptiness of the body can be contemplated by contemplating the emptiness of the body as a composition of a head, a torso, and limbs.

The body is empty. The body is devoid of inherent existence. The emptiness of the body can be contemplated by contemplating the emptiness of the body as a composition of solids, liquids, and gases.

The body is empty. The body is devoid of inherent existence. The emptiness of the body can be contemplated by contemplating the emptiness of the body as a composition of dust particles.

A sentient being is empty. A sentient being is devoid of inherent existence. The emptiness of a sentient being can be contemplated by contemplating the emptiness of a sentient being as a composition of the five skandhas.

# The emptiness of the five skandhas

## The emptiness of form

The mind perceives the presence of form. Form is the first skandha. Form is matter. The five skandhas are form, feeling, thinking, volition, and consciousness. Form is an entity. Form is perceived to be endowed with inherent existence. To perceive form to be endowed with inherent existence is to perceive form to exist independently from everything else. To perceive form to be endowed with inherent existence is to perceive form as a separate and distinct entity. Form is form endowed with inherent existence. Form and the inherent existence indwelling in form are inseparable.

The Buddha teaches that all is empty. The Buddha teaches that all is devoid of inherent existence. Form is empty. Form is devoid of inherent existence. The emptiness of form is the absence of inherent existence form is perceived to be endowed with. From the emptiness of form follows the fundamental absence of form. Form is fundamentally absent. Form has never come into existence. That which is fundamentally absent is not. Form is not. Form is not form. That which is fundamentally absent is inexpressible. Form is inexpressible. The emptiness and fundamental absence of form are the true nature of form.

Form perceived by the mind is the notion of form fabricated by the mind. Inherent existence form is perceived to be endowed with is the notion of inherent existence fabricated by the mind. The presence of the notion of form and the presence of the notion of inherent existence cause the perception of form endowed with inherent existence. It is by way of the notion of inherent existence that form is perceived to exist independently from everything else. It is by way of the notion of inherent existence that form is perceived as a separate and distinct entity. The fierceness of the arising of the notion of form is the mind's compulsion to fabricate the notion of form.

The emptiness and fundamental absence of form are revealed in the absence of the notion of form and the absence of the notion of inherent existence. The absence of the notion of form and the absence of the notion of inherent existence are the absence of form perceived to exist inherently and the absence of inherent existence form is perceived to be endowed with. The absence of inherent existence form is perceived to be endowed with is the emptiness of form. The absence of the notion of form and the absence of the notion of inherent existence are arrived at by detaching from the notion of form.

To detach from the notion of form is to not entertain the notion of form. To detach from the notion of form is to discontinue the formation of the notion of form. To detach from the notion of form is to seek the immediate absence of the notion of form. To detach from the notion of form is to withstand the fierceness of the arising of the notion of form. To detach from the notion of form is to endure patiently the absence of the notion of form. To detach from the notion of form is to detach from notions that say, "my body." To detach from the notion of form is to reveal the emptiness and fundamental absence of form.

### The emptiness of feeling

The mind perceives the presence of feeling. Feeling is the second skandha. The five skandhas are form, feeling, thinking, volition, and consciousness. Feeling is an entity. Feeling is perceived to be endowed with inherent existence. To perceive feeling to be endowed with inherent existence is to perceive feeling to exist independently from everything else. To perceive feeling to be endowed with inherent existence is to perceive feeling as a separate and distinct entity. Feeling is feeling endowed with inherent existence. Feeling and the inherent existence indwelling in feeling are inseparable.

The Buddha teaches that all is empty. The Buddha teaches that all is devoid of inherent existence. Feeling is empty. Feeling is devoid of inherent existence. The emptiness of feeling is the absence of inherent existence feeling is perceived to be endowed with. From the emptiness of feeling follows the fundamental absence of feeling. Feeling is fundamentally absent. Feeling has never come into existence. That which is fundamentally absent is not. Feeling is not. Feeling is not feeling. That which is fundamentally absent is inexpressible. Feeling is inexpressible. The emptiness and fundamental absence of feeling are the true nature of feeling.

Feeling perceived by the mind is the notion of feeling fabricated by the mind. Inherent existence feeling is perceived to be endowed with is the notion of inherent existence fabricated by the mind. The presence of the notion of feeling and the presence of the notion of inherent existence cause the perception of feeling endowed with inherent existence. It is by way of the notion of inherent existence that feeling is perceived to exist independently from everything else. It is by way of the notion of inherent existence that feeling is perceived as a separate and distinct entity. The fierceness of the arising of the notion of feeling is the mind's compulsion to fabricate the notion of feeling.

The emptiness and fundamental absence of feeling are revealed in the absence of the notion of feeling and the absence of the notion of inherent existence. The absence of the notion of feeling and the absence of the notion of inherent existence are the absence of feeling perceived to exist inherently and the absence of inherent existence feeling is perceived to be endowed with. The absence of inherent existence feeling is perceived to be endowed with is the emptiness of feeling. The absence of the notion of feeling and the absence of the notion of inherent existence are arrived at by detaching from the notion of feeling.

To detach from the notion of feeling is to not entertain the notion of feeling. To detach from the notion of feeling is to discontinue the formation of the notion of feeling. To detach from the notion of feeling is to seek the immediate absence of the notion of feeling. To detach from the notion of feeling is to withstand the fierceness of the arising of the notion of feeling. To detach from the notion of feeling is to endure patiently the absence of the notion of feeling. To detach from the notion of feeling is to detach from notions that say, "my feelings." To detach from the notion of feeling is to reveal the emptiness and fundamental absence of feeling.

## The emptiness of thinking

The mind perceives the presence of thinking. Thinking is the third skandha. The five skandhas are form, feeling, thinking, volition, and consciousness. Thinking is an entity. Thinking is perceived to be endowed with inherent existence. To perceive thinking to be endowed with inherent existence is to perceive thinking to exist independently from everything else. To perceive thinking to be endowed with inherent existence is to perceive thinking as a separate and distinct entity. Thinking is thinking endowed with inherent existence. Thinking and the inherent existence indwelling in thinking are inseparable.

The Buddha teaches that all is empty. The Buddha teaches that all is devoid of inherent existence. Thinking is empty. Thinking is devoid of inherent existence. The emptiness of thinking is the absence of inherent existence thinking is perceived to be endowed with. From the emptiness of thinking follows the fundamental absence of thinking. Thinking is fundamentally absent. Thinking has never come into existence. That which is fundamentally absent is not. Thinking is not. Thinking is not thinking. That which is fundamentally absent is inexpressible. Thinking is inexpressible. The emptiness and fundamental absence of thinking are the true nature of thinking.

Thinking perceived by the mind is the notion of thinking fabricated by the mind. Inherent existence thinking is perceived to be endowed with is the notion of inherent existence fabricated by the mind. The presence of the notion of thinking and the presence of the notion of inherent existence cause the perception of thinking endowed with inherent existence. It is by way of the notion of inherent existence that thinking is perceived to exist independently from everything else. It is by way of the notion of inherent existence that thinking is perceived as a separate and distinct entity. The fierceness of the arising of the notion of thinking is the mind's compulsion to fabricate the notion of thinking.

The emptiness and fundamental absence of thinking are revealed in the absence of the notion of thinking and the absence of the notion of inherent existence. The absence of the notion of thinking and the absence

141

of the notion of inherent existence are the absence of thinking perceived to exist inherently and the absence of inherent existence thinking is perceived to be endowed with. The absence of inherent existence thinking is perceived to be endowed with is the emptiness of thinking. The absence of the notion of thinking and the absence of the notion of inherent existence are arrived at by detaching from the notion of thinking.

To detach from the notion of thinking is to not entertain the notion of thinking. To detach from the notion of thinking is to discontinue the formation of the notion of thinking. To detach from the notion of thinking is to seek the immediate absence of the notion of thinking. To detach from the notion of thinking is to withstand the fierceness of the arising of the notion of thinking. To detach from the notion of thinking is to endure patiently the absence of the notion of thinking. To detach from the notion of thinking is to detach from notions that say, "my thoughts." To detach from the notion of thinking is to reveal the emptiness and fundamental absence of thinking.

### The emptiness of volition

The mind perceives the presence of volition. Volition is the fourth skandha. The five skandhas are form, feeling, thinking, volition, and consciousness. Volition is an entity. Volition is perceived to be endowed with inherent existence. To perceive volition to be endowed with inherent existence is to perceive volition to exist independently from everything else. To perceive volition to be endowed with inherent existence is to perceive volition as a separate and distinct entity. Volition is volition endowed with inherent existence. Volition and the inherent existence indwelling in volition are inseparable.

The Buddha teaches that all is empty. The Buddha teaches that all is devoid of inherent existence. Volition is empty. Volition is devoid of inherent existence. The emptiness of volition is the absence of inherent existence volition is perceived to be endowed with. From the emptiness of volition follows the fundamental absence of volition. Volition is fundamentally absent. Volition has never come into existence. That which is fundamentally absent is not. Volition is not. Volition is not volition. That which is fundamentally absent is inexpressible. Volition is inexpressible. The emptiness and fundamental absence of volition are the true nature of volition.

Volition perceived by the mind is the notion of volition fabricated by the mind. Inherent existence volition is perceived to be endowed with is the notion of inherent existence fabricated by the mind. The presence of the notion of volition and the presence of the notion of inherent existence cause the perception of volition endowed with inherent existence. It is by way of the notion of inherent existence that volition is perceived to exist independently from everything else. It is by way of the notion of inherent existence that volition is perceived as a separate and distinct entity. The fierceness of the arising of the notion of volition is the mind's compulsion to fabricate the notion of volition.

The emptiness and fundamental absence of volition are revealed in the absence of the notion of volition and the absence of the notion of inherent existence. The absence of the notion of volition and the absence of the notion of inherent existence are the absence of volition perceived to exist inherently and the absence of inherent existence volition is perceived to be endowed with. The absence of inherent existence volition is perceived to be endowed with is the emptiness of volition. The absence of the notion of volition and the absence of the notion of inherent existence are arrived at by detaching from the notion of volition.

To detach from the notion of volition is to not entertain the notion of volition. To detach from the notion of volition is to discontinue the formation of the notion of volition. To detach from the notion of volition is to seek the immediate absence of the notion of volition. To detach from the notion of volition is to withstand the fierceness of the arising of the notion of volition. To detach from the notion of volition is to endure patiently the absence of the notion of volition. To detach from the notion of volition is to detach from notions that say, "my will." To detach from the notion of volition is to reveal the emptiness and fundamental absence of volition.

### The emptiness of consciousness

The mind perceives the presence of consciousness. Consciousness is the fifth skandha. The five skandhas are form, feeling, thinking, volition, and consciousness. Consciousness is an entity. Consciousness is perceived to be endowed with inherent existence. To perceive consciousness to be endowed with inherent existence is to perceive consciousness to exist independently from everything else. To perceive consciousness to be endowed with inherent existence is to perceive consciousness as a separate and distinct entity. Consciousness is consciousness endowed with inherent existence. Consciousness and the inherent existence indwelling in consciousness are inseparable.

The Buddha teaches that all is empty. The Buddha teaches that all is devoid of inherent existence. Consciousness is empty. Consciousness is devoid of inherent existence. The emptiness of consciousness is the absence of inherent existence consciousness is perceived to be endowed with. From the emptiness of consciousness follows the fundamental absence of consciousness. Consciousness is fundamentally absent. Consciousness has never come into existence. That which is fundamentally absent is not. Consciousness is not. Consciousness is not consciousness. That which is fundamentally absent is inexpressible. Consciousness is inexpressible. The emptiness and fundamental absence of consciousness are the true nature of consciousness.

Consciousness perceived by the mind is the notion of consciousness fabricated by the mind. Inherent existence consciousness is perceived to be endowed with is the notion of inherent existence fabricated by the mind. The presence of the notion of consciousness and the presence of the notion of inherent existence cause the perception of consciousness endowed with inherent existence. It is by way of the notion of inherent existence that consciousness is perceived to exist independently from everything else. It is by way of the notion of inherent existence that consciousness is perceived as a separate and distinct entity. The fierceness of the arising of the notion of consciousness is the mind's compulsion to fabricate the notion of consciousness.

145

The emptiness and fundamental absence of consciousness are revealed in the absence of the notion of consciousness and the absence of the notion of inherent existence. The absence of the notion of consciousness and the absence of the notion of inherent existence are the absence of consciousness perceived to exist inherently and the absence of inherent existence consciousness is perceived to be endowed with. The absence of inherent existence consciousness is perceived to be endowed with is the emptiness of consciousness. The absence of the notion of consciousness and the absence of the notion of inherent existence are arrived at by detaching from the notion of consciousness.

To detach from the notion of consciousness is to not entertain the notion of consciousness. To detach from the notion of consciousness is to discontinue the formation of the notion of consciousness. To detach from the notion of consciousness is to seek the immediate absence of the notion of consciousness. To detach from the notion of consciousness is to withstand the fierceness of the arising of the notion of consciousness. To detach from the notion of consciousness is to endure patiently the absence of the notion of consciousness. To detach from the notion of consciousness is to detach from notions that say, "my consciousness." To detach from the notion of consciousness is to reveal the emptiness and fundamental absence of consciousness.

# The emptiness of the eighteen sense realms

## The emptiness of the first sense

The eye constitutes the first sense. Seeing is the coming together of the eye, form, and the consciousness of the eye. The eye is an entity. The eye is perceived to be endowed with inherent existence. It is perceived to exist by itself and in itself. The eye is an eye endowed with inherent existence.

The eye is empty. The eye is devoid of inherent existence. The emptiness of the eye is the absence of inherent existence the eye is perceived to be endowed with. From the emptiness of the eye follows the fundamental absence of the eye. The eye is empty and fundamentally absent. The emptiness and fundamental absence of the eye are the true nature of the eye.

The perception of the eye is caused by the presence of the notion of an eye. The perception of inherent existence is caused by the presence of the notion of inherent existence. The presence of the notion of an eye and the presence of the notion of inherent existence cause the perception of an inherently existent eye.

The emptiness and fundamental absence of the eye are revealed in the absence of the notion of an eye and the absence of the notion of inherent existence. The absence of the notion of an eye and the absence of the notion of inherent existence are arrived at by detaching from the notion of an eye.

To detach from the notion of an eye is to not entertain the notion of an eye. To detach from the notion of an eye is to cease the formation of the notion of an eye. To detach from the notion of an eye is to withstand the fierceness of the arising of the notion of an eye. To detach from the notion of an eye is to endure patiently the absence of the notion of an eye.

The eye is empty and fundamentally absent and so are the ear, the nose, the tongue, and the body.

### The emptiness of the first sense object

Form constitutes the first sense object. Seeing is the coming together of the eye, form, and the consciousness of the eye. Form is an entity. Form is perceived to be endowed with inherent existence. It is perceived to exist by itself and in itself. Form is form endowed with inherent existence.

Form is empty. Form is devoid of inherent existence. The emptiness of form is the absence of inherent existence form is perceived to be endowed with. From the emptiness of form follows the fundamental absence of form. Form is empty and fundamentally absent. The emptiness and fundamental absence of form are the true nature of form.

The perception of form is caused by the presence of the notion of form. The perception of inherent existence is caused by the presence of the notion of inherent existence. The presence of the notion of form and the presence of the notion of inherent existence cause the perception of form endowed with inherent existence.

The emptiness and fundamental absence of form are revealed in the absence of the notion of form and the absence of the notion of inherent existence. The absence of the notion of form and the absence of the notion of inherent existence are arrived at by detaching from the notion of form.

To detach from the notion of form is to not entertain the notion of form. To detach from the notion of form is to cease the formation of the notion of form. To detach from the notion of form is to withstand the fierceness of the arising of the notion of form. To detach from the notion of form is to endure patiently the absence of the notion of form.

Form is empty and fundamentally absent and so are sound, smell, taste, and touch.

## The emptiness of the first sense consciousness

The consciousness of the eye constitutes the first sense consciousness. Seeing is the coming together of the eye, form, and the consciousness of the eye. The consciousness of the eye is an entity. The consciousness of the eye is perceived to be endowed with inherent existence. It is perceived to exist by itself and in itself. The consciousness of the eye is a consciousness of the eye endowed with inherent existence.

The consciousness of the eye is empty. The consciousness of the eye is devoid of inherent existence. The emptiness of the consciousness of the eye is the absence of inherent existence the consciousness of the eye is perceived to be endowed with. From the emptiness of the consciousness of the eye follows the fundamental absence of the consciousness of the eye. The consciousness of the eye is empty and fundamentally absent.

The perception of the consciousness of the eye is caused by the presence of the notion of the consciousness of the eye. The perception of inherent existence is caused by the presence of the notion of inherent existence. The presence of the notion of the consciousness of the eye and the presence of the notion of inherent existence cause the perception of a consciousness of the eye endowed with inherent existence.

The emptiness and fundamental absence of the consciousness of the eye are revealed in the absence of the notion of the consciousness of the eye and the absence of the notion of inherent existence. The absence of the notion of the consciousness of the eye and the absence of the notion of inherent existence are arrived at by detaching from the notion of the consciousness of the eye.

To detach from the notion of the consciousness of the eye is to not entertain the notion of the consciousness of the eye. To detach from the notion of the consciousness of the eye is to withstand the fierceness of the notion of the consciousness of the eye. To detach from the notion of the consciousness of the eye is to endure patiently the absence of the notion of the consciousness of the eye.

The consciousness of the eye is empty and fundamentally absent and so are the consciousness of the ear, the consciousness of the nose, the consciousness of the tongue, and the consciousness of the body.

### The emptiness of the sixth sense

The mind constitutes the sixth sense. Thinking and feeling are the coming together of the mind, notions, and the consciousness of the mind. The mind is an entity. The mind is perceived to be endowed with inherent existence. It is perceived to exist by itself and in itself. The mind is a mind endowed with inherent existence.

The mind is empty. The mind is devoid of inherent existence. The emptiness of the mind is the absence of inherent existence the mind is perceived to be endowed with. From the emptiness of the mind follows the fundamental absence of the mind. The mind is empty and fundamentally absent. The emptiness and fundamental absence of the mind are the true nature of the mind.

The perception of the mind is caused by the presence of the notion of a mind. The perception of inherent existence is caused by the presence of the notion of inherent existence. The presence of the notion of a mind and the presence of the notion of inherent existence cause the perception of an inherently existent mind.

The emptiness and fundamental absence of the mind are revealed in the absence of the notion of a mind and the absence of the notion of inherent existence. The absence of the notion of a mind and the absence of the notion of inherent existence are arrived at by detaching from the notion of a mind.

To detach from the notion of a mind is to not entertain the notion of a mind. To detach from the notion of a mind is to cease the formation of the notion of a mind. To detach from the notion of a mind is to withstand the fierceness of the arising of the notion of a mind. To detach from the notion of a mind is to endure patiently the absence of the notion of a mind.

## The emptiness of the sixth sense object

Notions constitute the sixth sense object. Thinking and feeling are the coming together of the mind, notions, and the consciousness of the mind. A notion is an entity. A notion is perceived to be endowed with inherent existence. It is perceived to exist by itself and in itself. Notions are notions endowed with inherent existence.

Notions are empty. Notions are devoid of inherent existence. The emptiness of notions is the absence of inherent existence notions are perceived to be endowed with. From the emptiness of notions follows the fundamental absence of notions. Notions are empty and fundamentally absent. The emptiness and fundamental absence of notions are the true nature of notions.

The perception of notions is caused by the presence of the notion of notions. The perception of inherent existence is caused by the presence of the notion of inherent existence. The presence of the notion of notions and the presence of the notion of inherent existence cause the perception of inherently existent notions.

The emptiness and fundamental absence of notions are revealed in the absence of the notion of notions and the absence of the notion of inherent existence. The absence of the notion of notions and the absence of the notion of inherent existence are arrived at by detaching from the notion of notions.

To detach from the notion of notions is to not entertain the notion of notions. To detach from the notion of notions is to cease the formation of the notion of notions. To detach from the notion of notions is to withstand the fierceness of the arising of the notion of notions. To detach from the notion of notions is to endure patiently the absence of the notion of notions.

## The emptiness of the sixth sense consciousness

The consciousness of the mind constitutes the sixth sense consciousness. Thinking and feeling are the coming together of the mind, notions, and the consciousness of the mind. The consciousness of the mind is an entity. The consciousness of the mind is perceived to be endowed with inherent existence. It is perceived to exist by itself and in itself. The consciousness of the mind is a consciousness of the mind endowed with inherent existence.

The consciousness of the mind is empty. The consciousness of the mind is devoid of inherent existence. The emptiness of the consciousness of the mind is the absence of inherent existence the consciousness of the mind is perceived to be endowed with. From the emptiness of the consciousness of the mind follows the fundamental absence of the consciousness of the mind. The consciousness of the mind is empty and fundamentally absent.

The perception of the consciousness of the mind is caused by the presence of the notion of the consciousness of the mind. The perception of inherent existence is caused by the presence of the notion of inherent existence. The presence of the notion of the consciousness of the mind and the presence of the notion of inherent existence cause the perception of a consciousness of the mind endowed with inherent existence.

The emptiness and fundamental absence of the consciousness of the mind are revealed in the absence of the notion of the consciousness of the mind and the absence of the notion of inherent existence. The absence of the notion of the consciousness of the mind and the absence of the notion of inherent existence are arrived at by detaching from the notion of the consciousness of the mind.

To detach from the notion of the consciousness of the mind is to not entertain the notion of the consciousness of the mind. To detach from the notion of the consciousness of the mind is to withstand the fierceness of the notion of the consciousness of the mind. To detach from the notion of the consciousness of the mind is to endure patiently the absence of the notion of the consciousness of the mind.

# The five skandhas and eighteen sense realms

### The five skandhas

The five skandhas are empty and fundamentally absent. Form is empty and fundamentally absent. Feeling is empty and fundamentally absent. Thinking is empty and fundamentally absent. Volition is empty and fundamentally absent. Consciousness is empty and fundamentally absent. All is empty and fundamentally absent.

### The eighteen sense realms

The eighteen sense realms are empty and fundamentally absent. The eye, the ear, the nose, the tongue, the body, and the mind are empty and fundamentally absent. Form, sound, smell, taste, touch, and notions are empty and fundamentally absent. The consciousness of the eye, the consciousness of the ear, the consciousness of the nose, the consciousness of the tongue, the consciousness of the body, and the consciousness of the mind are empty and fundamentally absent. The six senses are empty and fundamentally absent. The six sense objects are empty and fundamentally absent. The six sense consciousnesses are empty and fundamentally absent. The eighteen sense realms are empty and fundamentally absent. All is empty and fundamentally absent.

# The self is a name

### The self is a name

The self perceived by the mind is the notion of self fabricated by the mind. The notion of self arises from the mind. The mind is that which gives rise to the notion of self. The notion of self is merely a name. The self perceived by the mind is merely a name.

A name cannot exist independently from everything else. A name cannot exist by itself and in itself. A name is empty. It is devoid of inherent existence. The emptiness of a name is the absence of inherent existence a name is perceived to be endowed with. From the emptiness of a name follows the fundamental absence of a name. A name devoid of inherent existence is not a name. A name devoid of inherent existence is not. Names are empty and fundamentally absent.

The self perceived by the mind is the notion of self fabricated by the mind. The notion of self is merely a name. The self perceived by the mind is merely a name. Names are empty and fundamentally absent. The self is empty and fundamentally absent.

### The self is a composition of names

The self is a composition of form, feeling, thinking, volition, and consciousness. Form perceived by the mind is the notion of form fabricated by the mind. The notion of form is merely a name. Form perceived by the mind is merely a name. Feeling perceived by the mind is the notion of feeling fabricated by the mind. The notion of feeling is merely a name. Feeling perceived by the mind is merely a name. Thinking perceived by the mind is the notion of thinking fabricated by the mind. The notion of thinking is merely a name. Thinking perceived by the mind is merely a name. Volition perceived by the mind is the notion of volition fabricated by the mind. The notion of volition is merely a name. Volition perceived by the mind is merely a name. Consciousness perceived by the mind is the notion of consciousness fabricated by the mind. The notion of consciousness is merely a name. Consciousness perceived by the mind is merely a name. The self is a composition of form, feeling, thinking, volition, and consciousness. Form, feeling, thinking, volition, and consciousness are merely names. The self is a composition of names. Names are empty and fundamentally absent. The self is a composition of that which is empty and fundamentally absent. A composition of that which is empty and fundamentally absent is empty and fundamentally absent. The self is empty and fundamentally absent.

### The self is a name of names

The self perceived by the mind is the notion of self fabricated by the mind. The notion of self is merely a name. The self perceived by the mind is merely a name. The self is a name attached to the composition of form, feeling, thinking, volition, and consciousness. Form perceived by the mind is the notion of form fabricated by the mind. Feeling perceived by the mind is the notion of feeling fabricated by the mind. Thinking perceived by the mind is the notion of thinking fabricated by the mind. Volition perceived by the mind is the notion of volition fabricated by the mind. Consciousness perceived by the mind is the notion of consciousness fabricated by the mind. Notions of entities are merely names. Form, feeling, thinking, volition, and consciousness are merely names. The self is a name attached to the composition of form, feeling, thinking, volition, and consciousness. The self is a name attached to a composition of names. The self is a name of names. Names are empty and fundamentally absent. A name of names is empty and fundamentally absent. The self is empty and fundamentally absent.

155

# Detachment from the notion of self

### Detachment from the notion of self

The self is empty and fundamentally absent. The emptiness and fundamental absence of the self are the true nature of the self. The emptiness and fundamental absence of the self are revealed by cultivating detachment from the notion of self.

To withstand the fierceness of the arising of the notion of self is to cultivate detachment from the notion of self. To withstand the fierceness of the arising of the notion of form, feeling, thinking, volition, and consciousness is to cultivate detachment from the notion of self.

To endure patiently the absence of the notion of self is to cultivate detachment from the notion of self. To endure patiently the absence of the notion of form, feeling, thinking, volition, and consciousness is to cultivate detachment from the notion of self.

To detach from notions such as "I" and "mine" is to cultivate detachment from the notion of self. To detach from notions such as "my body, my feelings, my thoughts, my will, and my consciousness" is to cultivate detachment from the notion of self.

### Detachment from arbitrary and false names

The self perceived by the mind is the notion of self fabricated by the mind. The notion of self is an arbitrary and false name. To detach from the notion of self is to detach from an arbitrary and false name. To withstand the fierceness of the notion of self is to withstand the fierceness of an arbitrary and false name.

Form perceived by the mind is the notion of form fabricated by the mind. The notion of form is an arbitrary and false name. To detach from the notion of form is to detach from an arbitrary and false name. To withstand the fierceness of the notion of form is to withstand the fierceness of an arbitrary and false name.

Feeling perceived by the mind is the notion of feeling fabricated by the mind. The notion of feeling is an arbitrary and false name. To detach from the notion of feeling is to detach from an arbitrary and false name. To withstand the fierceness of the notion of feeling is to withstand the fierceness of an arbitrary and false name.

Thinking perceived by the mind is the notion of thinking fabricated by the mind. The notion of thinking is an arbitrary and false name. To detach from the notion of thinking is to detach from an arbitrary and false name. To withstand the fierceness of the notion of thinking is to withstand the fierceness of an arbitrary and false name.

Volition perceived by the mind is the notion of volition fabricated by the mind. The notion of volition is an arbitrary and false name. To detach from the notion of volition is to detach from an arbitrary and false name. To withstand the fierceness of the notion of volition is to withstand the fierceness of an arbitrary and false name.

Consciousness perceived by the mind is the notion of consciousness fabricated by the mind. The notion of consciousness is an arbitrary and false name. To detach from the notion of consciousness is to detach from an arbitrary and false name. To withstand the fierceness of the notion of consciousness is to withstand the fierceness of an arbitrary and false name.


### Detachment from the notion of inherent existence

The notion of self comes into being in the presence of the notion of inherent existence. To withstand the fierceness of the notion of self is to withstand the fierceness of the notion of inherent existence.

The notion of form comes into being in the presence of the notion of inherent existence. To withstand the fierceness of the notion of form is to withstand the fierceness of the notion of inherent existence.

The notion of feeling comes into being in the presence of the notion of inherent existence. To withstand the fierceness of the notion of feeling is to withstand the fierceness of the notion of inherent existence.

The notion of thinking comes into being in the presence of the notion of inherent existence. To withstand the fierceness of the notion of thinking is to withstand the fierceness of the notion of inherent existence.

The notion of volition comes into being in the presence of the notion of inherent existence. To withstand the fierceness of the notion of volition is to withstand the fierceness of the notion of inherent existence.

The notion of consciousness comes into being in the presence of the notion of inherent existence. To withstand the fierceness of the notion of consciousness is to withstand the fierceness of the notion of inherent existence.

# The body is a name

## The body is a name

The body perceived by the mind is the notion of a body fabricated by the mind. The notion of a body arises from the mind. The mind is that which gives rise to the notion of a body. The notion of a body is merely a name. The body perceived by the mind is merely a name.

A name cannot exist independently from everything else. A name cannot exist by itself and in itself. A name is empty. It is devoid of inherent existence. The emptiness of a name is the absence of inherent existence a name is perceived to be endowed with. From the emptiness of a name follows the fundamental absence of a name. A name devoid of inherent existence is not a name. A name devoid of inherent existence is not. Names are empty and fundamentally absent.

The body perceived by the mind is the notion of a body fabricated by the mind. The notion of a body is merely a name. The body perceived by the mind is merely a name. Names are empty and fundamentally absent. The body is empty and fundamentally absent.

## The body is a composition of names

The body is a composition of a head, a torso, and limbs. The head perceived by the mind is the notion of a head fabricated by the mind. The notion of a head is merely a name. The head perceived by the mind is merely a name. The torso perceived by the mind is the notion of a torso fabricated by the mind. The notion of a torso is merely a name. The torso perceived by the mind is merely a name. A limb perceived by the mind is the notion of a limb fabricated by the mind. The notion of a limb is merely a name. A limb perceived by the mind is merely a name. The body is a composition of a head, a torso, and limbs. The head, the torso, and the limbs are merely names. The body is a composition of names. Names are empty and fundamentally absent. The body is a composition of that which is empty and fundamentally absent. A composition of that

159

which is empty and fundamentally absent is empty and fundamentally absent. The body is empty and fundamentally absent.


## The body is a name of names

The body perceived by the mind is the notion of a body fabricated by the mind. The notion of a body is merely a name. The body perceived by the mind is merely a name. The body is a name attached to the composition of a head, a torso, and limbs. The head perceived by the mind is the notion of a head fabricated by the mind. The torso perceived by the mind is the notion of a torso fabricated by the mind. The limbs perceived by the mind are notions of limbs fabricated by the mind. Notions of entities are merely names. The head, the torso, and the limbs are merely names. The body is a name attached to the composition of a head, a torso, and limbs. The body is a name attached to a composition of names. The body is a name of names. Names are empty and fundamentally absent. A name of names is empty and fundamentally absent. The body is empty and fundamentally absent.

# Detachment from the notion of a body

## Detachment from the notion of a body

The body is empty and fundamentally absent. The emptiness and fundamental absence of the body are the true nature of the body. The emptiness and fundamental absence of the body are revealed by cultivating detachment from the notion of a body.

To withstand the fierceness of the arising of the notion of a body is to cultivate detachment from the notion of a body. To withstand the fierceness of the arising of the notion of a head, a torso, arms, hands, legs, and feet is to cultivate detachment from the notion of a body.

To endure patiently the absence of the notion of a body is to cultivate detachment from the notion of a body. To endure patiently the absence of the notion of a head, a torso, arms, hands, legs, and feet is to cultivate detachment from the notion of a body.

## Detachment from arbitrary and false names

The body perceived by the mind is the notion of a body fabricated by the mind. The notion of a body is an arbitrary and false name. To detach from the notion of a body is to detach from an arbitrary and false name. To withstand the fierceness of the notion of a body is to withstand the fierceness of an arbitrary and false name.

The head perceived by the mind is the notion of a head fabricated by the mind. The notion of a head is an arbitrary and false name. To detach from the notion of a head is to detach from an arbitrary and false name. To withstand the fierceness of the notion of a head is to withstand the fierceness of an arbitrary and false name.

The torso perceived by the mind is the notion of a torso fabricated by the mind. The notion of a torso is an arbitrary and false name. To detach from the notion of a torso is to detach from an arbitrary and false name. To withstand the fierceness of the notion of a torso is to withstand the fierceness of an arbitrary and false name.

A limb perceived by the mind is the notion of a limb fabricated by the mind. The notion of a limb is an arbitrary and false name. To detach from the notion of a limb is to detach from an arbitrary and false name. To withstand the fierceness of the notion of a limb is to withstand the fierceness of an arbitrary and false name.

### Detachment from the notion of inherent existence

The notion of a body comes into being in the presence of the notion of inherent existence. To withstand the fierceness of the notion of a body is to withstand the fierceness of the notion of inherent existence.

The notion of a head comes into being in the presence of the notion of inherent existence. To withstand the fierceness of the notion of a head is to withstand the fierceness of the notion of inherent existence.

The notion of a torso comes into being in the presence of the notion of inherent existence. To withstand the fierceness of the notion of a torso is to withstand the fierceness of the notion of inherent existence.

The notion of a limb comes into being in the presence of the notion of inherent existence. To withstand the fierceness of the notion of a limb is to withstand the fierceness of the notion of inherent existence.

# The emptiness of a lifespan

## The emptiness of life

The mind perceives the presence of life. The mind perceives the presence of a living being. A living being is that which is endowed with life. The life of a living being is an entity. The life of a living being is perceived to be endowed with inherent existence. To perceive life to be endowed with inherent existence is to perceive life to exist independently from everything else. To perceive life to be endowed with inherent existence is to perceive life as a separate and distinct entity. A living being is an entity. A living being is perceived to be endowed with inherent existence. To perceive a living being to be endowed with inherent existence is to perceive a living being to exist independently from everything else. To perceive a living being to be endowed with inherent existence is to perceive a living being as a separate and distinct entity. The life of a living being is an inherently existent entity. A living being endowed with life is an inherently existent entity.

All is empty. All is devoid of inherent existence. The life of a living being is empty. The life of a living being is devoid of inherent existence. The emptiness of life is the absence of inherent existence life is perceived to be endowed with. From the emptiness of life follows the fundamental absence of life. The life of a living being is empty and fundamentally absent. Such an entity has never come into existence. All is empty. All is devoid of inherent existence. A living being endowed with life is empty. A living being endowed with life is devoid of inherent existence. The emptiness of a living being is the absence of inherent existence a living being is perceived to be endowed with. From the emptiness of a living being follows the fundamental absence of a living being. A living being is empty and fundamentally absent. Such an entity has never come into existence. The life of a living being and a living being endowed with life are empty and fundamentally absent.

All is mind. The life of a living being perceived by the mind is the notion of life fabricated by the mind. Inherent existence life is perceived to be endowed with is the notion of inherent existence fabricated by the mind. It is by way of the notion of inherent existence that life is perceived as a separate and distinct entity. The presence of the notion of life and the presence of the notion of inherent existence cause the perception of life endowed with inherent existence. All is mind. A living being perceived by the mind is the notion of a living being fabricated by the mind. Inherent existence a living being is perceived to be endowed with is the notion of inherent existence fabricated by the mind. It is by way of the notion of inherent existence that a living being is perceived as a separate and distinct entity. The presence of the notion of a living being and the presence of the notion of inherent existence cause the perception of a living being endowed with inherent existence.

The life of a living being is empty and fundamentally absent. The emptiness and fundamental absence of life are revealed in the absence of the notion of life and the absence of the notion of inherent existence. The absence of the notion of life and the absence of the notion of inherent existence are the absence of life perceived to exist inherently and the absence of inherent existence life is perceived to be endowed with. A living being is empty and fundamentally absent. The emptiness and fundamental absence of a living being are revealed in the absence of the notion of a living being and the absence of the notion of inherent existence. The absence of the notion of a living being and the absence of the notion of inherent existence are the absence of a living being perceived to exist inherently and the absence of inherent existence a living being is perceived to be endowed with.

The absence of the notion of life and the absence of the notion of inherent existence are arrived at by detaching from the notion of life. To detach from the notion of life is to endure patiently the absence of the notion of life. The absence of the notion of a living being and the absence of the notion of inherent existence are arrived at by detaching from the notion of a living being. To detach from the notion of a living being is to endure patiently the absence of the notion of a living being. To detach from the notion of life and the notion of a living being is to detach from notions that say, "my life" and "my existence." To detach from the notion of a living being and the notion of life is to detach from notions that say, "I live" and "I exist." To detach from the notion of life is to reveal the emptiness and fundamental absence of life. To detach from the notion of a living being is to reveal the emptiness and fundamental absence of a living being.

### The emptiness of a lifespan

The mind perceives the presence of a lifespan. The mind perceives the presence of a living being. A lifespan is the period of time of life between birth and death. A living being is that which is endowed with such a lifespan. To perceive a living being and a lifespan is to perceive a living being existing in the past, present, and future. To perceive a lifespan and a living being is to perceive the past, present, and future of a living being. A lifespan is an entity. A lifespan is perceived to be endowed with inherent existence. To perceive a lifespan to be endowed with inherent existence is to perceive a lifespan to exist independently from everything else. A living being is an entity. A living being is perceived to be endowed with inherent existence. To perceive a living being to be endowed with inherent existence is to perceive a living being as a separate and distinct entity. A lifespan is a lifespan endowed with inherent existence. A living being is a living being endowed with inherent existence.

All is empty. All is devoid of inherent existence. A lifespan is empty. A lifespan is devoid of inherent existence. The emptiness of a lifespan is the absence of inherent existence a lifespan is perceived to be endowed with. From the emptiness of a lifespan follows the fundamental absence of a lifespan. A lifespan is empty and fundamentally absent. All is empty. All is devoid of inherent existence. A living being is empty. A living being is devoid of inherent existence. The emptiness of a living being is the absence of inherent existence a living being is perceived to be endowed with. From the emptiness of a living being follows the fundamental absence of a living being. A living being is empty and fundamentally absent. The period of time of life between birth and death is empty and fundamentally absent. A living being existing in the past, present, and future is empty and fundamentally absent. The past, present, and future of a living being are empty and fundamentally absent.

All is mind. A lifespan perceived by the mind is the notion of a lifespan fabricated by the mind. Inherent existence a lifespan is perceived to be endowed with is the notion of inherent existence fabricated by the mind. It is by way of the notion of inherent existence that a lifespan is perceived to exist independently from everything else. All is mind. A living being perceived by the mind is the notion of a living being fabricated by the mind. Inherent existence a living being is perceived to be endowed with is the notion of inherent existence fabricated by the mind. It is by way of the notion of inherent existence that a living being is perceived as a separate and distinct entity. The perception of a living being existing in the past, present, and future arises from the notion of a living being and the notion of a lifespan. The perception of the past, present, and future of a living being arises from the notion of a lifespan and the notion of a living being.

A lifespan is empty and fundamentally absent. The emptiness and fundamental absence of a lifespan are revealed in the absence of the notion of a lifespan and the absence of the notion of inherent existence. The absence of the notion of a lifespan and the absence of the notion of inherent existence are the absence of a lifespan perceived to exist inherently and the absence of inherent existence a lifespan is perceived to be endowed with. A living being is empty and fundamentally absent. The emptiness and fundamental absence of a living being are revealed in the absence of the notion of a living being and the absence of the notion of inherent existence. The absence of the notion of a living being and the absence of the notion of inherent existence are the absence of a living being perceived to exist inherently and the absence of inherent existence a living being is perceived to be endowed with.

The absence of the notion of a lifespan and the absence of the notion of inherent existence are arrived at by detaching from the notion of a lifespan. The absence of the notion of a living being and the absence

166

of the notion of inherent existence are arrived at by detaching from the notion of a living being. To detach from the notion of a living being and the notion of a lifespan is to detach from the notion of a living being existing in the past, present, and future. To detach from the notion of a living being existing in the past, present, and future is to detach from notions that say, "I was in the past," "I am in the present," and "I will be in the future." To detach from the notion of a lifespan and the notion of a living being is to detach from the notion of the past, present, and future of a living being. To detach from the notion of the past, present, and future of a living being is to detach from notions that say, "my life in the past," "my life in the present," and "my life in the future."

### The emptiness of a lifespan

The mind perceives the presence of a lifespan. The mind perceives the presence of a living being. A lifespan is the endless continuation of birth and death. A living being is that which is endowed with such a lifespan. A living being is that which is perceived to undergo the endless continuation of birth and death. A living being is that which is perceived to wander in samsara. A living being is that which is perceived to depart from a body upon death and enter another body upon formation. A lifespan is an entity. A lifespan is perceived to be endowed with inherent existence. To perceive a lifespan to be endowed with inherent existence is to perceive a lifespan to exist independently from everything else. A living being is an entity. A living being is perceived to be endowed with inherent existence. To perceive a living being to be endowed with inherent existence is to perceive a living being as a separate and distinct entity. A lifespan is a lifespan endowed with inherent existence. A living being is a living being endowed with inherent existence.

All is empty. All is devoid of inherent existence. A lifespan is empty. A lifespan is devoid of inherent existence. The emptiness of a lifespan is the absence of inherent existence a lifespan is perceived to be endowed with. From the emptiness of a lifespan follows the fundamental absence of a lifespan. A lifespan is empty and fundamentally absent. All is empty. All is devoid of inherent existence. A living being is empty. A living being is devoid of inherent existence. The emptiness of a living being is the absence of inherent existence a living being is perceived to be endowed with. From the emptiness of a living being follows the fundamental absence of a living being. A living being is empty and fundamentally absent. The endless continuation of birth and death is empty and fundamentally absent. A living being undergoing the endless continuation of birth and death is empty and fundamentally absent. A living being wandering in samsara is empty and fundamentally absent. A living being departing from a body upon death and entering another body upon formation is empty and fundamentally absent. A lifespan and a living being are empty and fundamentally absent. Such entities have never come into existence.

All is mind. A lifespan perceived by the mind is the notion of a lifespan fabricated by the mind. Inherent existence a lifespan is perceived to be endowed with is the notion of inherent existence fabricated by the mind. It is by way of the notion of inherent existence that a lifespan is perceived to exist independently from everything else. All is mind. A living being perceived by the mind is the notion of a living being fabricated by the mind. Inherent existence a living being is perceived to be endowed with is the notion of inherent existence fabricated by the mind. It is by way of the notion of inherent existence that a living being is perceived as a separate and distinct entity. The perception of a living being undergoing an endless continuation of birth and death arises from the notion of a living being and the notion of a lifespan. The perception of a living being wandering in samsara arises from the notion of a living being and the notion of a lifespan. The perception of a living being departing from a body upon death and entering another body upon formation arises from the notion of a living being and the notion of a lifespan.

A lifespan is empty and fundamentally absent. The emptiness and fundamental absence of a lifespan are revealed in the absence of the notion of a lifespan and the absence of the notion of inherent existence. The absence of the notion of a lifespan and the absence of the notion of inherent existence are the absence of a lifespan perceived to exist inherently and the absence of inherent existence a lifespan is perceived to be endowed with. The absence of inherent existence a lifespan is perceived to be endowed with is the emptiness of a lifespan. A living being is empty and fundamentally absent. The emptiness and fundamental absence of a living being are revealed in the absence of the notion of a living being and the absence of the notion of inherent existence. The absence of the notion of a living being and the absence of the notion of inherent existence are the absence of a living being perceived to exist inherently and the absence of inherent existence a living being is perceived to be endowed with. The absence of inherent existence a living being is perceived to be endowed with is the emptiness of a living being.

The absence of the notion of a lifespan and the absence of the notion of inherent existence are arrived at by detaching from the notion of a lifespan. To detach from the notion of a lifespan is to endure patiently the absence of the notion of a lifespan. The absence of the notion of a living being and the absence of the notion of inherent existence are arrived at by detaching from the notion of a living being. To detach from the notion of a living being is to endure patiently the absence of the notion of a living being. To detach from the notion of a living being and the notion of a lifespan is to detach from the notion of a living being undergoing an endless continuation of birth and death. To detach from the notion of a living being and the notion of a lifespan is to detach from the notion of a living being wandering in samsara. To detach from the notion of a living being and the notion of a lifespan is to detach from the notion of a living being departing from a body upon death and entering another body upon formation. To detach from the notion of a lifespan is to reveal the emptiness and fundamental absence of a lifespan. To detach from the notion of a living being is to reveal the emptiness and fundamental absence of a living being.

# Four notions

### Four notions

The Diamond Sutra says, "A bodhisattva who entertains the notion of self, the notion of a person, the notion of a sentient being, or the notion of a lifespan is not a bodhisattva." The notion of self, the notion of a person, the notion of a sentient being, and the notion of a lifespan are the four notions of the Diamond Sutra.

### Unsurpassed complete enlightenment

The Diamond Sutra says, "Unsurpassed complete enlightenment is attained by cultivating all virtues in the absence of the notion of self, a person, a sentient being, and a lifespan." The end of ignorance is the end of suffering. The end of ignorance is unsurpassed complete enlightenment. Unsurpassed complete enlightenment is the end of suffering.

### The notion of self

The Diamond Sutra says, "A bodhisattva who entertains the notion of self, the notion of a person, the notion of a sentient being, or the notion of a lifespan is not a bodhisattva." The word 'self' has two different meanings. The word 'self' means 'I'. The word 'self' also means 'inherent existence'. To be endowed with inherent existence is to exist independently from everything else. To be endowed with inherent existence is to exist by itself and in itself. Entities are entities endowed with inherent existence. Entities are entities endowed with a self. The term 'notion of self' from the Diamond Sutra can therefore mean 'notion of self' as well as 'notion of inherent existence'. To not entertain the notion of self is to not entertain the notion of self or the notion of inherent existence. To abide in the absence of the notion of self is to abide in the absence of the notion of self and the absence of the notion of inherent existence.

## The notion of self

The mind perceives the presence of entities. Entities perceived by the mind are perceived to be endowed with a self. To perceive an entity to be endowed with a self is to perceive an entity to exist by itself and in itself. An entity is an entity endowed with a self. An entity and the self indwelling in an entity are inseparable.

All is empty. To be empty is to be devoid of a self. Emptiness is the absence of a self. The emptiness of entities is the absence of a self entities are perceived to be endowed with. From the emptiness of entities follows the fundamental absence of entities. Entities devoid of a self are not entities. Entities devoid of a self are not.

Entities perceived by the mind are notions of entities fabricated by the mind. A self entities are perceived to be endowed with is the notion of self fabricated by the mind. The perception of entities endowed with a self is caused by the presence of notions of entities and the presence of the notion of self.

The emptiness and fundamental absence of entities are revealed in the absence of notions of entities and the absence of the notion of self. The absence of notions of entities and the absence of the notion of self are the absence of entities perceived to exist by and in themselves and the absence of a self entities are perceived to be endowed with.

The absence of notions of entities and the absence of the notion of self are arrived at by detaching from the notion of self. To detach from the notion of self is to withstand the fierceness of the arising of the notion of self. To detach from the notion of self is to endure patiently the absence of the notion of self.

## The notion of self

The self is a self endowed with a self. The self is empty. The self is devoid of a self. The emptiness of the self is the absence of a self the self is perceived to be endowed with. The perception of a self is caused by the presence of the notion of self. The emptiness of the self is revealed in the absence of the notion of self. To detach from the notion of self is to arrive at the absence of the notion of self. To detach from the notion of self is to reveal the emptiness of the self.

A person is a person endowed with a self. A person is empty. A person is devoid of a self. The emptiness of a person is the absence of a self a person is perceived to be endowed with. The perception of a self is caused by the presence of the notion of self. The emptiness of a person is revealed in the absence of the notion of self. To detach from the notion of self is to arrive at the absence of the notion of self. To detach from the notion of self is to reveal the emptiness of a person.

A sentient being is a sentient being endowed with a self. A sentient being is empty. A sentient being is devoid of a self. The emptiness of a sentient being is the absence of a self a sentient being is perceived to be endowed with. The perception of a self is caused by the presence of the notion of self. The emptiness of a sentient being is revealed in the absence of the notion of self. To detach from the notion of self is to arrive at the absence of the notion of self. To detach from the notion of self is to reveal the emptiness of a sentient being.

A lifespan is a lifespan endowed with a self. A lifespan is empty. A lifespan is devoid of a self. The emptiness of a lifespan is the absence of a self a lifespan is perceived to be endowed with. The perception of a self is caused by the presence of the notion of self. The emptiness of a lifespan is revealed in the absence of the notion of self. To detach from the notion of self is to arrive at the absence of the notion of self. To detach from the notion of self is to reveal the emptiness of a lifespan.

### The notion of a person

The Diamond Sutra says, "A bodhisattva who entertains the notion of self, the notion of a person, the notion of a sentient being, or the notion of a lifespan is not a bodhisattva." The word 'person' has two different meanings. The word 'person' means 'human being'. The word 'person' also means 'others'. The term 'notion of a person' from the Diamond Sutra can therefore mean 'notion of a human being' as well as 'notion of others'. The four notions of the Diamond Sutra can be applied to the self as well as to others. The aforementioned sentence from the Diamond Sutra can therefore be understood as follows, "A bodhisattva who entertains the notion of inherent existence, the notion of self, the notion of a human being pertaining to the self, the notion of a sentient being pertaining to the self, or the notion of a lifespan pertaining to the self is not a bodhisattva." The aforementioned sentence from the Diamond Sutra can therefore also be understood as follows, "A bodhisattva who entertains the notion of inherent existence, the notion of others, the notion of a human being pertaining to others, the notion of a sentient being pertaining to others, or the notion of a lifespan pertaining to others is not a bodhisattva."

### The notion of a person

Detachment from the notion of a human being is detachment from the notion of a person. Detachment from the notion of a man is detachment from the notion of a person. Detachment from the notion of a woman is detachment from the notion of a person. Detachment from the notion of others is detachment from the notion of a person. Detachment from the notion of people is detachment from the notion of a person.

### The notion of a sentient being

The Diamond Sutra says, "A bodhisattva who entertains the notion of self, the notion of a person, the notion of a sentient being, or the notion of a lifespan is not a bodhisattva." The word 'sentient being' has different meanings. A sentient being is that which is composed of the five skandhas. A sentient being is that which arises from the five skandhas. The five skandhas are form, feeling, thinking, volition, and consciousness. A sentient being is that which is defiled by the afflictions. A sentient being is that which is plagued by the afflictions. The afflictions are ignorance, desire, and hatred. A sentient being is that which is reborn again and again in samsara. A sentient being is that which suffers in samsara since time without beginning. Samsara is the endless cycle of birth and death. A sentient being is that which is at this shore. A sentient being is that which has not been ferried across to the other shore. This shore is ignorance and samsara. The other shore is enlightenment and nirvana.

### The notion of a sentient being

Detachment from the notion of form is detachment from the notion of a sentient being. Detachment from the notion of feeling is detachment from the notion of a sentient being. Detachment from the notion of thinking is detachment from the notion of a sentient being. Detachment from the notion of volition is detachment from the notion of a sentient being. Detachment from the notion of consciousness is detachment from the notion of a sentient being.

### The notion of a sentient being

Form is the first skandha. Form is matter. The body of oneself pertains to and arises from form. The body of others pertains to and arises from form. To detach from the notion of a sentient being is to detach from the notion of form. To detach from the notion of a sentient being is to detach from the notion of a body pertaining to the self. To detach from the notion of a sentient being is to detach from the notion of a body pertaining to others.


### The notion of a lifespan

The Diamond Sutra says, "A bodhisattva who entertains the notion of self, the notion of a person, the notion of a sentient being, or the notion of a lifespan is not a bodhisattva." The word 'lifespan' refers to a lifespan as well as to that which is endowed with a lifespan. That which is endowed with a lifespan is a living being. The word 'lifespan' has different meanings.

First, the word 'lifespan' can refer to the life of a living being and to a living being endowed with life. To detach from the notion of a lifespan is to detach from notions that say, "my life" and "my existence." To detach from the notion of a lifespan is to detach from notions that say, "I live" and "I exist."

Second, a 'lifespan' can refer to the period of time of life between birth and death and to a living being endowed with such a lifespan. To detach from the notion of a lifespan is to detach from notions that say, "I was in the past," "I am in the present," and "I will be in the future." To detach from the notion of a lifespan is to detach from notions that say, "my life in the past," "my life in the present," and "my life in the future."

Third, a 'lifespan' can refer to the endless continuation of birth and death and to a living being endowed with such a lifespan. To detach from the notion of a lifespan is to detach from the notion of an entity undergoing an endless continuation of birth and death. To detach from the notion of a lifespan is to detach from the notion of an entity wandering in samsara.

### The notion of a lifespan

A living being is that which is endowed with life. A living being is that which is endowed with a lifespan. That which is perceived to be endowed with life is the self. That which is perceived to be endowed with a lifespan is the self. The term 'living being' refers to the self. The self is a living being.

### Four names

The self perceived by the mind is the notion of self fabricated by the mind. The notion of self is an arbitrary and false name. To detach from the notion of self is to detach from an arbitrary and false name. To not entertain the notion of self is to not entertain an arbitrary and false name.

A person perceived by the mind is the notion of a person fabricated by the mind. The notion of a person is an arbitrary and false name. To detach from the notion of a person is to detach from an arbitrary and false name. To not entertain the notion of a person is to not entertain an arbitrary and false name.

A sentient being perceived by the mind is the notion of a sentient being fabricated by the mind. The notion of a sentient being is an arbitrary and false name. To detach from the notion of a sentient being is to detach from an arbitrary and false name. To not entertain the notion of a sentient being is to not entertain an arbitrary and false name.

A lifespan perceived by the mind is the notion of a lifespan fabricated by the mind. The notion of a lifespan is an arbitrary and false name. To detach from the notion of a lifespan is to detach from an arbitrary and false name. To not entertain the notion of a lifespan is to not entertain an arbitrary and false name.

# The Diamond Sutra

## Upholding the Diamond Sutra

The Diamond Sutra is the Sutra of the Perfection of Diamond Wisdom. The Diamond Sutra is a sutra on the perfection of wisdom. The perfection of wisdom is the cultivation of wisdom. Wisdom is understanding the true nature of all. The emptiness and fundamental absence of entities are the true nature of all. The emptiness and fundamental absence of entities are revealed by cultivating detachment from the notion of inherent existence. The emptiness and fundamental absence of entities are revealed by cultivating detachment from all notions of entities. To cultivate detachment from the notion of inherent existence and all notions of entities is to cultivate the perfection of wisdom. To cultivate detachment from the notion of inherent existence and all notions of entities is to uphold the Diamond Sutra.

## Diamond wisdom

The Diamond Sutra is the Sutra of the Perfection of Diamond Wisdom. Wisdom is like a diamond that cuts through the shroud of ignorance. Ignorance is the perception of that which is fundamentally absent. Inherently existent entities are fundamentally absent. Ignorance is the perception of inherently existent entities. Ignorance is the perception of a self, a person, a sentient being, and a lifespan.

Wisdom is detachment from the notion of inherent existence and all notions of entities. To detach from the notion of inherent existence and all notions of entities is to cease the perception of inherently existent entities. To detach from the notion of inherent existence and all notions of entities is to cut through the shroud of ignorance. Wisdom is like a diamond that cuts through the shroud of ignorance.

### Unsurpassed complete enlightenment

The Diamond Sutra is the Sutra of the Perfection of Diamond Wisdom. The perfection of wisdom is the cultivation of wisdom. To cultivate the perfection of wisdom is to shatter the affliction of ignorance. To cultivate detachment from the notion of inherent existence and all notions of entities is to shatter the affliction of ignorance. The end of ignorance is the end of suffering. The end of ignorance is unsurpassed complete enlightenment. Unsurpassed complete enlightenment is the end of suffering. To uphold the Diamond Sutra is to cultivate the way leading to the end of ignorance. To uphold the Diamond Sutra is to cultivate the way leading to the end of suffering.

# Virtue

### Virtue

The bodhisattva way encompasses the cultivation of virtue. Virtue is that which benefits and enlightens self and others. To observe the five precepts is to cultivate virtue. To uphold the ten virtues is to cultivate virtue. To accomplish the six perfections is to cultivate virtue.

### The five precepts

The five precepts are the abstention from killing, stealing, sexual misconduct, lying, and intoxication. To observe the five precepts is to cultivate virtue. To observe the five precepts is to cultivate the bodhisattva way.

### The ten virtues

The ten virtues are the abstention from the ten evils. The ten evils are killing, stealing, sexual misconduct, false speech, divisive speech, malicious speech, frivolous speech, greed, anger, and false views. To abstain from the ten evils is to cultivate virtue. To abstain from the ten evils is to cultivate the bodhisattva way.

### The six perfections

The six perfections are the perfection of giving, discipline, endurance, vigor, meditation, and wisdom. To accomplish the six perfections is to cultivate virtue. To accomplish the six perfections is to cultivate the bodhisattva way.

### The perfection of wisdom

The perfection of wisdom is the cultivation of wisdom. Wisdom is understanding the true nature of all. The emptiness and fundamental absence of entities are the true nature of all. The emptiness and fundamental absence of entities are revealed by cultivating detachment from the notion of inherent existence and all notions of entities. To cultivate detachment from the notion of inherent existence and all notions of entities is to cultivate the perfection of wisdom.


### Virtue and wisdom

The bodhisattva way encompasses the cultivation of virtue and wisdom. Virtue is that which benefits and enlightens self and others. Wisdom is understanding the true nature of all. The emptiness and fundamental absence of entities are the true nature of all. Virtue and wisdom can be cultivated separately. Virtue and wisdom can also be cultivated together. Virtue and wisdom are cultivated together by cultivating virtue in the absence of the notion of inherent existence. Virtue and wisdom are cultivated together by cultivating virtue in the absence of all notions of entities. The Diamond Sutra says, "Unsurpassed complete enlightenment is attained by cultivating all virtues in the absence of the notion of self, a person, a sentient being, and a lifespan."


### Giving and wisdom

The bodhisattva way encompasses the perfection of giving and the perfection of wisdom. The perfection of giving is the cultivation of benevolent giving. The perfection of wisdom is the cultivation of wisdom. Wisdom is understanding the true nature of all. The emptiness and fundamental absence of entities are the true nature of all. The perfection of giving and the perfection of wisdom can be cultivated separately. The perfection of giving and the perfection of wisdom can also be cultivated together. The perfection of giving and the perfection of wisdom are cultivated together by cultivating giving in the absence of the notion of inherent existence. The perfection of giving and the perfection of wisdom are cultivated together by cultivating giving in the absence of all notions of entities.

### Giving and wisdom

The bodhisattva way encompasses the perfection of giving and the perfection of wisdom. The perfection of giving and the perfection of wisdom can be cultivated together. The perfection of giving and the perfection of wisdom are cultivated together by cultivating giving in the absence of the notion of self. The absence of the notion of self is arrived at by detaching from the notion of self. The three essentials for cultivating detachment from the notion of self are mindfulness, awareness, and endurance. Mindfulness is presence of mind. Awareness is awareness of the presence of the notion of self. Endurance is endurance of the absence of the notion of self. To cultivate giving in the absence of the notion of self is to cultivate both the perfection of giving and the perfection of wisdom.

### Giving and wisdom

The bodhisattva way encompasses the perfection of giving and the perfection of wisdom. The perfection of giving and the perfection of wisdom can be cultivated together. The perfection of giving and the perfection of wisdom are cultivated together by cultivating giving in the absence of the notion of people. The absence of the notion of people is arrived at by detaching from the notion of people. The three essentials for cultivating detachment from the notion of people are mindfulness, awareness, and endurance. Mindfulness is presence of mind. Awareness is awareness of the presence of the notion of people. Endurance is endurance of the absence of the notion of people. To cultivate giving in the absence of the notion of people is to cultivate both the perfection of giving and the perfection of wisdom.

### Giving and wisdom

The bodhisattva way encompasses the perfection of giving and the perfection of wisdom. The perfection of giving and the perfection of wisdom can be cultivated together. The perfection of giving and the perfection of wisdom are cultivated together by cultivating giving in the absence of the notion of inherent existence. The absence of the notion of inherent existence is arrived at by detaching from the notion of inherent existence. The three essentials for cultivating detachment from the notion of inherent existence are mindfulness, awareness, and endurance. Mindfulness is presence of mind. Awareness is awareness of the presence of the notion of inherent existence. Endurance is endurance of the absence of the notion of inherent existence. To cultivate giving in the absence of the notion of inherent existence is to cultivate both the perfection of giving and the perfection of wisdom.

### Giving and wisdom

The bodhisattva way encompasses the perfection of giving and the perfection of wisdom. The perfection of giving is the cultivation of benevolent giving. The perfection of wisdom is the cultivation of wisdom. Wisdom is understanding the true nature of the self. Wisdom is understanding the true nature of all. The absence of the self is the true nature of the self. The absence of inherent existence is the true nature of all. To cultivate the perfection of giving is to cultivate virtue and merit. To cultivate the perfection of wisdom is to cultivate virtue and merit. Virtue is the cause. Merit is the effect. The Diamond Sutra says, " 'Subhuti, if a bodhisattva filled as many worlds as the sands in the Ganges River with the seven treasures and gave them away benevolently. If another bodhisattva understood that all is devoid of a self and that all is devoid of inherent existence and attained patient endurance thereof, the merits attained by this bodhisattva would surpass the merits attained by the former bodhisattva. Why? Subhuti, bodhisattvas do not accept the merits they attain.' Subhuti said to the Buddha, 'World Honored One, why do bodhisattvas not accept merits?' 'Subhuti, bodhisattvas are not attached to the merits they attain. Bodhisattvas therefore do not accept the merits they attain.' "

# Emptiness

## Emptiness

Emptiness is the absence of inherent existence. Emptiness is also the absence of the notion of inherent existence. Emptiness as the absence of inherent existence is the emptiness of entities. The emptiness of entities is a quality of entities. The absence of inherent existence is a quality of entities. To be empty is to be devoid of inherent existence. The emptiness of entities can be contemplated and reflected on. To contemplate the emptiness of compositions is to contemplate the emptiness of entities. The emptiness of entities can be understood conceptually. To understand the impossibility of compositions to be endowed with inherent existence is to understand the emptiness of entities conceptually. The emptiness of entities can also be understood intuitively.

Emptiness as the absence of the notion of inherent existence is a state of mind. Emptiness as the absence of the notion of inherent existence is the state of emptiness. The state of emptiness cannot be contemplated or reflected on. The state of emptiness can only be abided in. To abide in the absence of the notion of inherent existence is to abide in the state of emptiness. To abide in the state of emptiness is to understand the emptiness of entities intuitively. To understand the emptiness of entities intuitively is to realize the sudden or gradual absence of inherent existence, which is caused by the sudden or gradual absence of the notion of inherent existence. To understand the emptiness of entities intuitively is to arrive at the state of emptiness. The state of emptiness reveals the emptiness of entities.

### Understanding

To understand the emptiness of entities is to not entertain the notion of inherent existence. To not entertain the notion of inherent existence is to understand the emptiness of entities.

To detach from the notion of inherent existence is to not attain anything whatsoever. To not attain anything whatsoever is to detach from the notion of inherent existence.

To understand the emptiness of entities is to not attain anything whatsoever. To not attain anything whatsoever is to understand the emptiness of entities.

### The notion of inherent existence

The extent to which the notion of inherent existence is entertained is the extent to which inherent existence is perceived. The extent to which the notion of inherent existence is not entertained is the extent to which the absence of inherent existence is revealed.

The extent to which the notion of inherent existence is entertained is the extent to which the emptiness of entities is shrouded. The extent to which the notion of inherent existence is not entertained is the extent to which the emptiness of entities is revealed.

### Perception

The extent to which inherent existence is perceived is the extent to which emptiness is shrouded. The extent to which inherent existence is not perceived is the extent to which emptiness is revealed.

The extent to which an entity is perceived is the extent to which emptiness is shrouded. The extent to which an entity is not perceived is the extent to which emptiness is revealed.

## In emptiness

The mind perceives the presence of inherently existent entities. The perception of an inherently existent entity is caused by the presence of the notion of an entity and the presence of the notion of inherent existence. The notion of an entity comes into being in the presence of the notion of inherent existence. The arising of the notion of an entity is dependent on the presence of the notion of inherent existence. The notion of an entity does not come into being in the absence of the notion of inherent existence. The absence of the notion of inherent existence is the absence of the notion of an entity. The absence of the notion of inherent existence is the absence of all notions of entities. To abide in the absence of the notion of inherent existence is to abide in the absence of the notion of inherent existence and the absence of all notions of entities. The absence of the notion of inherent existence is the absence of the perception of inherently existent entities.

# People

### The perception of people

The mind perceives the presence of people. People are fundamentally absent. People perceived by the mind are the notion of people fabricated by the mind. The mind perceives that which is fundamentally absent, because it fabricates a notion of that which is fundamentally absent.

### The fundamental absence of people

The fundamental absence of people is revealed by cultivating detachment from the notion of people. To cultivate detachment from the notion of people is to withstand again and again the fierceness of the arising of the notion of people. To cultivate detachment from the notion of people is to endure again and again the absence of the notion of people.

### All is devoid of people

Form and sound are devoid of people. The ten directions are devoid of people. The three times are devoid of people. All is devoid of people.

### The notion of people

People perceived in the presence of people are not different from people perceived in the absence of people. People perceived in the presence of people are the notion of people fabricated by the mind. People perceived in the absence of people are the notion of people fabricated by the mind. Form is pure and quiescent. Form is devoid of people.

# Desire and hatred

## The cause of suffering

Sentient beings suffer in samsara since time without beginning. Suffering has a cause. The afflictions are the cause of suffering. The afflictions are ignorance, desire, and hatred. Suffering can be ceased. Suffering is ceased by ceasing the cause of suffering. Suffering is ceased by ceasing ignorance, desire, and hatred. To cease suffering, the affliction of ignorance must be ceased. To cease suffering, the affliction of desire and hatred must be ceased.

## Desire

Desire arises from the perception of entities. Desire arises from the perception of a self that harbors desire. Desire arises from the perception of things, people, and circumstances towards which desire is harbored. Desire is desire by an entity for an entity.

Desire does not come into being in the absence of the perception of entities. Desire does not arise in the absence of the perception of a self. It does not arise in the absence of the perception of things, people, and circumstances.

## Hatred

Hatred arises from the perception of entities. Hatred arises from the perception of a self that harbors hatred. Hatred arises from the perception of things, people, and circumstances towards which hatred is harbored. Hatred is hatred by an entity for an entity.

Hatred does not come into being in the absence of the perception of entities. Hatred does not arise in the absence of the perception of a self. It does not arise in the absence of the perception of things, people, and circumstances.

### Ignorance

Desire and hatred arise from ignorance. Desire and hatred arise from the perception of entities. Entities are fundamentally absent. Entities have never come into existence. The perception of entities is the perception of that which is fundamentally absent. Ignorance is the perception of that which is fundamentally absent. Ignorance is the perception of entities. Desire and hatred arise from the perception of entities. Desire and hatred arise from ignorance.

### Wisdom

Desire and hatred arise from ignorance. Desire and hatred do not arise in the absence of ignorance. The absence of ignorance is the absence of desire and hatred.

Wisdom is the absence of ignorance. Desire and hatred do not arise in the presence of wisdom. The presence of wisdom is the absence of desire and hatred.

### The cessation of the afflictions

Ignorance gives rise to desire and hatred. Desire and hatred give rise to ignorance. To cease desire and hatred, the affliction of ignorance must be ceased. To cease ignorance, the affliction of desire and hatred must be ceased.

# Desire and lust

## Desire and lust

Sentient beings suffer in samsara since time without beginning. Suffering can be ceased. Suffering is ceased by ceasing the cause of suffering. Suffering is ceased by ceasing ignorance, desire, and hatred. To cease suffering, the affliction of ignorance must be ceased. To cease suffering, the affliction of desire and lust must be ceased. Desire and lust can be ceased in four ways. First, desire and lust can be ceased by not exposing the body and mind to worldly dusts. Second, desire and lust can be ceased by detaching from desire and lust. Third, desire and lust can be ceased by detaching from the notion of self, the notion of a person, and the notion of a body. Fourth, desire and lust can be ceased by detaching from the notion of inherent existence.

## Worldly dusts

Desire and lust can be ceased by not exposing the body and mind to worldly dusts. Desire and lust arises in the presence of worldly dusts. Desire and lust arises in the absence of worldly dusts. To tame desire and lust is to discontinue the formation of desire and lust. To tame desire and lust is to withstand the fierceness of the arising of desire and lust. The fierceness of the arising of desire and lust is the mind's incessant compulsion to give rise to desire and lust. Desire and lust in the absence of worldly dusts is difficult to tame yet tamable. Desire and lust in the presence of worldly dusts is untamable. That which can be tamed must be tamed. That which is untamable must be averted. To not expose the body and mind to worldly dusts is to avert desire and lust in the presence of worldly dusts. To not expose the body and mind to worldly dusts is to avert that which is untamable. Not exposing the body and mind to worldly dusts is the foundation of the way. Exposing the body and mind to worldly dusts is the absence of the way. Desire and lust can be ceased by not exposing the body and mind to worldly dusts.

### Detachment from desire and lust

Desire and lust can be ceased by detaching from desire and lust. To detach from desire and lust is to discontinue the formation of desire and lust. To detach from desire and lust is to seek the immediate absence of desire and lust. To detach from desire and lust is to withstand the fierceness of the arising of desire and lust. To detach from desire and lust is to endure patiently the absence of desire and lust.

### Mindfulness, awareness, and endurance

Desire and lust can be ceased by detaching from desire and lust. To detach from desire and lust is to discontinue the formation of desire and lust. To detach from desire and lust is to cultivate mindfulness, awareness, and endurance. Mindfulness is presence of mind. Awareness is awareness of the presence of desire and lust. Endurance is endurance of the absence of desire and lust.

### Mindfulness of the Buddha

Desire and lust can be ceased by detaching from desire and lust. To be mindful of the Buddha is to detach from desire and lust. To be mindful of the Buddha is to think of the name of the Buddha. The presence of the name of the Buddha is the absence of desire and lust, for the mind can only perceive one notion at a time.

### Lascivious thoughts

Desire and lust arises in the presence of lascivious thoughts. Desire and lust can be ceased by ceasing the formation of lascivious thoughts. The absence of lascivious thoughts is the absence of desire and lust.

To be mindful of the Buddha is to cease the formation of lascivious thoughts. The presence of the name of the Buddha is the absence of lascivious thoughts, for the mind can only entertain one thought at a time.

## Detachment from the notion of self, a person, and a body

Desire and lust can be ceased by detaching from the notion of self, the notion of a person, and the notion of a body. The formation of desire and lust is caused by the perception of a self, the perception a person, and the perception of a body. Desire is desire by an entity for an entity. The perception of a self is the perception of an entity. The perception of a person is the perception of an entity. The perception of a body is the perception of an entity. The perception of an entity is caused by the presence of the notion of an entity. The perception of an entity does not come into being in the absence of the notion of an entity.

The perception of a self is caused by the presence of the notion of self. The perception of a self does not come into being in the absence of the notion of self. The absence of the notion of self is the absence of the perception of a self. The perception of a person is caused by the presence of the notion of a person. The perception of a person does not come into being in the absence of the notion of a person. The absence of the notion of a person is the absence of the perception of a person. The perception of a body is caused by the presence of the notion of a body. The perception of a body does not come into being in the absence of the notion of a body. The absence of the notion of a body is the absence of the perception of a body.

Desire and lust does not arise in the absence of the perception of a self, a person, and a body. Desire and lust does not arise in the absence of the notion of self, a person, and a body. The absence of the notion of self, a person, and a body are the absence of the perception of a self, a person, and a body. The absence of the notion of self, a person, and a body are the absence of desire and lust. Detachment from the notion of self, a person, and a body is detachment from desire and lust. Desire and lust can be ceased by detaching from the notion of self, the notion of a person, and the notion of a body.

## Detachment from the notion of inherent existence

Desire and lust can be ceased by detaching from the notion of inherent existence. The formation of desire and lust is caused by the presence of the notion of self, the presence of the notion of a person, and the presence of the notion of a body. Each notion of an entity comes into being in the presence of the notion of inherent existence. The arising of the notion of an entity is dependent on the arising and presence of the notion of inherent existence. The notion of an entity does not come into being in the absence of the notion of inherent existence.

The notion of self does not come into being in the absence of the notion of inherent existence. The absence of the notion of inherent existence is the absence of the notion of self. The notion of a person does not come into being in the absence of the notion of inherent existence. The absence of the notion of inherent existence is the absence of the notion of a person. The notion of a body does not come into being in the absence of the notion of inherent existence. The absence of the notion of inherent existence is the absence of the notion of a body.

Desire and lust does not arise in the absence of the notion of self, a person, and a body. Desire and lust does not arise in the absence of the notion of inherent existence. The absence of the notion of inherent existence is the absence of the notion of self, a person, and a body. The absence of the notion of inherent existence is the absence of desire and lust. Detachment from the notion of inherent existence is detachment from desire and lust. Desire and lust can be ceased by detaching from the notion of inherent existence.

# Anger and hatred

## Anger and hatred

Sentient beings suffer in samsara since time without beginning. Suffering can be ceased. Suffering is ceased by ceasing the cause of suffering. Suffering is ceased by ceasing ignorance, desire, and hatred. To cease suffering, the affliction of ignorance must be ceased. To cease suffering, the affliction of anger and hatred must be ceased. Anger and hatred can be ceased in three ways. First, anger and hatred can be ceased by detaching from anger and hatred. Second, anger and hatred can be ceased by detaching from the notion of self, the notion of a person, and the notion of a circumstance. Third, anger and hatred can be ceased by detaching from the notion of inherent existence.

## Detachment from anger and hatred

Anger and hatred can be ceased by detaching from anger and hatred. To detach from anger and hatred is to discontinue the formation of anger and hatred. To detach from anger and hatred is to seek the immediate absence of anger and hatred. To detach from anger and hatred is to withstand the fierceness of the arising of anger and hatred. To detach from anger and hatred is to endure patiently the absence of anger and hatred.

## Mindfulness, awareness, and endurance

Anger and hatred can be ceased by detaching from anger and hatred. To detach from anger and hatred is to discontinue the formation of anger and hatred. To detach from anger and hatred is to cultivate mindfulness, awareness, and endurance. Mindfulness is presence of mind. Awareness is awareness of the presence of anger and hatred. Endurance is endurance of the absence of anger and hatred.

## Mindfulness of the Buddha

Anger and hatred can be ceased by detaching from anger and hatred. To be mindful of the Buddha is to detach from anger and hatred. To be mindful of the Buddha is to think of the name of the Buddha. The presence of the name of the Buddha is the absence of anger and hatred, for the mind can only perceive one notion at a time.

## Detachment from notions of entities

Anger and hatred can be ceased by detaching from the notion of self, the notion of a person, and the notion of a circumstance. The formation of anger and hatred is caused by the perception of a self, the perception a person, and the perception of a circumstance. Hatred is hatred by an entity for an entity. The perception of a self is the perception of an entity. The perception of a person is the perception of an entity. The perception of a circumstance is the perception of an entity. The perception of an entity is caused by the presence of the notion of an entity. The perception of an entity does not come into being in the absence of the notion of an entity.

The perception of a self is caused by the presence of the notion of self. The perception of a self does not come into being in the absence of the notion of self. The absence of the notion of self is the absence of the perception of a self. The perception of a person is caused by the presence of the notion of a person. The perception of a person does not come into being in the absence of the notion of a person. The absence of the notion of a person is the absence of the perception of a person. The perception of a circumstance is caused by the presence of the notion of a circumstance. The perception of a circumstance does not come into being in the absence of the notion of a circumstance. The absence of the notion of a circumstance is the absence of the perception of a circumstance.

Anger and hatred do not arise in the absence of the perception of a self, a person, and a circumstance. Anger and hatred do not arise in the absence of the notion of self, a person, and a circumstance. The absence

195

of the notion of self, a person, and a circumstance are the absence of the perception of a self, a person, and a circumstance. The absence of the notion of self, a person, and a circumstance are the absence of anger and hatred. Detachment from the notion of self, a person, and a circumstance is detachment from anger and hatred. Anger and hatred can be ceased by detaching from the notion of self, the notion of a person, and the notion of a circumstance.

## Detachment from the notion of inherent existence

Anger and hatred can be ceased by detaching from the notion of inherent existence. The formation of anger and hatred is caused by the presence of the notion of self, the presence of the notion of a person, and the presence of the notion of a circumstance. Each notion of an entity comes into being in the presence of the notion of inherent existence. The arising of the notion of an entity is dependent on the presence of the notion of inherent existence. The notion of an entity does not come into being in the absence of the notion of inherent existence.

The notion of self does not come into being in the absence of the notion of inherent existence. The absence of the notion of inherent existence is the absence of the notion of self. The notion of a person does not come into being in the absence of the notion of inherent existence. The absence of the notion of inherent existence is the absence of the notion of a person. The notion of a circumstance does not come into being in the absence of the notion of inherent existence. The absence of the notion of inherent existence is the absence of the notion of a circumstance.

Anger and hatred do not arise in the absence of the notion of self, a person, and a circumstance. Anger and hatred do not arise in the absence of the notion of inherent existence. The absence of the notion of inherent existence is the absence of the notion of self, a person, and a circumstance. The absence of the notion of inherent existence is the absence of anger and hatred. Detachment from the notion of inherent existence is detachment from anger and hatred. Anger and hatred can be ceased by detaching from the notion of inherent existence.

# Arrogance

## Arrogance

Arrogance is the perception of a self being superior to others. Arrogance is an affliction. Suffering is ceased by ceasing the cause of suffering. Suffering is ceased by ceasing the afflictions. To cease suffering, the affliction of ignorance must be ceased. To cease suffering, the affliction of arrogance must be ceased. Arrogance can be ceased in three ways. First, arrogance can be ceased by detaching from arrogance. Second, arrogance can be ceased by detaching from the notion of self and the notion of others. Third, arrogance can be ceased by detaching from the notion of inherent existence.

## The fierceness of the notion of self

The self perceived by the mind is the notion of self fabricated by the mind. The mind has been fabricating the notion of self since time without beginning. The formation of the notion of self has become an incessant habit of mind. The notion of self arises fast. The notion of self arises fiercely. The fierceness of the arising of the notion of self is the mind's compulsion to fabricate the notion of self.

Arrogance is the perception of a self being superior to others. Arrogance strengthens the mind's compulsion to fabricate the notion of self. Arrogance strengthens the fierceness of the arising of the notion of self. To detach from and give up the affliction of arrogance is to cease the mind's compulsion to fabricate the notion of self. To detach from and give up the affliction of arrogance is to cease the fierceness of the arising of the notion of self.

### Detachment from arrogance

Arrogance can be ceased by detaching from arrogance. To detach from arrogance is to discontinue the formation of arrogance. To detach from arrogance is to seek the immediate absence of arrogance. To detach from arrogance is to withstand the fierceness of the arising of arrogance. To detach from arrogance is to endure patiently the absence of arrogance.

### Mindfulness, awareness, and endurance

Arrogance can be ceased by detaching from arrogance. To detach from arrogance is to discontinue the formation of arrogance. To detach from arrogance is to cultivate mindfulness, awareness, and endurance. Mindfulness is presence of mind. Awareness is awareness of the presence of arrogance. Endurance is endurance of the absence of arrogance.

### Detachment from the notion of self and others

Arrogance can be ceased by detaching from the notion of self and the notion of others. The formation of arrogance is caused by the perception of self and others. The perception of a self is the perception of an entity. The perception of others is the perception of an entity. The perception of an entity is caused by the presence of the notion of an entity. The perception of an entity does not come into being in the absence of the notion of an entity. The absence of the notion of an entity is the absence of the perception of an entity.

The perception of a self is caused by the presence of the notion of self. The perception of a self does not come into being in the absence of the notion of self. The absence of the notion of self is the absence of the perception of a self. The perception of others is caused by the presence of the notion of others. The perception of others does not come into being in the absence of the notion of others. The absence of the notion of others is the absence of the perception of others.

Arrogance does not arise in the absence of the perception of self and others. Arrogance does not arise in the absence of the notion of self and others. The absence of the notion of self and others are the absence of the perception of self and others. The absence of the notion of self and others are the absence of the affliction of arrogance. Detachment from the notion of self and others is detachment from the affliction of arrogance. Arrogance can be ceased by detaching from the notion of self and the notion of others.

## Detachment from the notion of inherent existence

Arrogance can be ceased by detaching from the notion of inherent existence. The formation of arrogance is caused by the presence of the notion of self and the presence of the notion of others. Each notion of an entity comes into being in the presence of the notion of inherent existence. The arising of the notion of an entity is dependent on the presence of the notion of inherent existence. The notion of an entity does not come into being in the absence of the notion of inherent existence.

The arising of the notion of self is dependent on the presence of the notion of inherent existence. The notion of self does not come into being in the absence of the notion of inherent existence. The absence of the notion of inherent existence is the absence of the notion of self. The arising of the notion of others is dependent on the presence of the notion of inherent existence. The notion of others does not come into being in the absence of the notion of inherent existence. The absence of the notion of inherent existence is the absence of the notion of others.

Arrogance does not arise in the absence of the notion of self and others. Arrogance does not arise in the absence of the notion of inherent existence. The absence of the notion of inherent existence is the absence of the notion of self and others. The absence of the notion of inherent existence is the absence of the affliction of arrogance. Detachment from the notion of inherent existence is detachment from the affliction of arrogance. Arrogance can be ceased by detaching from the notion of inherent existence.

### Severe flaw

Grasping at flaws and shortcomings of others is a severe flaw of the mind.

### Grave fault

Arguing and disputing in order to prevail over others is a grave fault of the mind.

# The emptiness of motion and positions

## The emptiness of the motion of walking

The mind perceives the motion of walking. That which is perceived to walk is a person. The motion of walking is an entity. The motion of walking is perceived to be endowed with inherent existence. To perceive the motion of walking to be endowed with inherent existence is to perceive the motion of walking to exist independently from everything else. To perceive the motion of walking to be endowed with inherent existence is to perceive the motion of walking to exist by itself and in itself. The motion of walking is a motion endowed with inherent existence. The motion of walking and the inherent existence indwelling in the motion of walking are inseparable.

The motion of walking is devoid of inherent existence. That which is perceived to walk is a person. The motion of walking is the motion of a moving person. The motion of walking is dependent on the moving person. The motion of walking cannot exist independently from the moving person. That which cannot exist independently from a person cannot exist independently from everything else. That which cannot exist independently from everything else cannot be endowed with inherent existence. That which cannot be endowed with inherent existence is devoid of inherent existence. The motion of walking is devoid of inherent existence.

The motion of walking is empty. The motion of walking is devoid of inherent existence. The emptiness of the motion of walking is the absence of inherent existence the motion of walking is perceived to be endowed with. From the emptiness of the motion of walking follows the fundamental absence of the motion of walking. The motion of walking is fundamentally absent. That which is fundamentally absent is not. The motion of walking is not. That which is fundamentally absent is inexpressible. The motion of walking is inexpressible. The emptiness and fundamental absence of the motion of walking are the true nature of the motion of walking.

The motion of walking perceived by the mind is the notion of walking fabricated by the mind. Inherent existence the motion of walking is perceived to be endowed with is the notion of inherent existence fabricated by the mind. The presence of the notion of walking and the presence of the notion of inherent existence cause the perception of walking endowed with inherent existence. It is by way of the notion of inherent existence that the motion of walking is perceived to exist independently from everything else. The fierceness of the arising of the notion of walking is the mind's compulsion to fabricate the notion of walking.

The emptiness and fundamental absence of the motion of walking are revealed in the absence of the notion of walking and the absence of the notion of inherent existence. The absence of the notion of walking and the absence of the notion of inherent existence are the absence of the motion of walking perceived to exist inherently and the absence of inherent existence the motion of walking is perceived to be endowed with. The absence of the notion of walking and the absence of the notion of inherent existence can be arrived at by detaching from the notion of walking or by detaching from the notion of a moving person.

The absence of the notion of walking and the absence of the notion of inherent existence can be arrived at by detaching from the notion of walking. To detach from the notion of walking is to not entertain the notion of walking. To detach from the notion of walking is to discontinue the formation of the notion of walking. To detach from the notion of walking is to seek the immediate absence of the notion of walking. To detach from the notion of walking is to withstand the fierceness of the arising of the notion of walking. To detach from the notion of walking is to endure patiently the absence of the notion of walking.

That which is perceived to walk is a person. The motion of walking is the motion of a moving person. The motion of walking perceived by the mind is the notion of walking fabricated by the mind. A moving person perceived by the mind is the notion of a person fabricated by the mind. The perception of walking is caused by the presence of the notion of a person and the presence of the notion of walking. The notion of walking comes into being in the presence of the notion of a person. The arising of the notion of walking is dependent on the presence of the notion of a person. The notion of walking does not come into being in the absence of the notion of a person.

The absence of the notion of walking and the absence of the notion of inherent existence can be arrived at by detaching from the notion of a moving person. To detach from the notion of a moving person is to detach from both the notion of a person and the notion of walking. The notion of walking does not come into being in the absence of the notion of a person. The absence of the notion of a person is the absence of the notion of a person and the absence of the notion of walking. To detach from the notion of a person is to withstand the fierceness of the arising of the notion of a person. To detach from the notion of a person is to endure patiently the absence of the notion of a person.

To detach from the notion of walking is to arrive at the absence of the notion of walking in the presence of the notion of a person. The absence of the notion of walking and the presence of the notion of a person are the presence of the perception of a person and the absence of the perception of walking. To detach from the notion of a person is to arrive at the absence of the notion of a person and the absence of the notion of walking. The absence of the notion of a person and the absence of the notion of walking are the absence of the perception of a person and the absence of the perception of walking.

## The emptiness of the position of standing

The mind perceives the position of standing. That which is perceived to stand is a person. The position of standing is an entity. The position of standing is perceived to be endowed with inherent existence. To perceive the position of standing to be endowed with inherent existence is to perceive the position of standing to exist independently from everything else. To perceive the position of standing to be endowed with inherent existence is to perceive the position of standing to exist by itself and in itself. The position of standing is a position endowed with inherent existence. The position of standing and the inherent existence indwelling in the position of standing are inseparable.

The position of standing is devoid of inherent existence. That which is perceived to stand is a person. The position of standing is the position of a standing person. The position of standing is dependent on the standing person. The position of standing cannot exist independently from the standing person. That which cannot exist independently from a person cannot exist independently from everything else. That which cannot exist independently from everything else cannot be endowed with inherent existence. That which cannot be endowed with inherent existence is devoid of inherent existence. The position of standing is devoid of inherent existence.

The position of standing is empty. The position of standing is devoid of inherent existence. The emptiness of the position of standing is the absence of inherent existence the position of standing is perceived to be endowed with. From the emptiness of the position of standing follows the fundamental absence of the position of standing. The position of standing is fundamentally absent. That which is fundamentally absent is not. The position of standing is not. That which is fundamentally absent is inexpressible. The position of standing is inexpressible. The emptiness and fundamental absence of the position of standing are the true nature of the position of standing.

The position of standing perceived by the mind is the notion of standing fabricated by the mind. Inherent existence the position of standing is perceived to be endowed with is the notion of inherent existence fabricated by the mind. The presence of the notion of standing and the presence of the notion of inherent existence cause the perception of standing endowed with inherent existence. It is by way of the notion of inherent existence that the position of standing is perceived to exist independently from everything else. The fierceness of the arising of the notion of standing is the mind's compulsion to fabricate the notion of standing.

The emptiness and fundamental absence of the position of standing are revealed in the absence of the notion of standing and the absence of the notion of inherent existence. The absence of the notion of standing and the absence of the notion of inherent existence are the absence of the position of standing perceived to exist inherently and the absence of inherent existence the position of standing is perceived to be endowed with. The absence of the notion of standing and the absence of the notion of inherent existence can be arrived at by detaching from the notion of standing or by detaching from the notion of a standing person.

The absence of the notion of standing and the absence of the notion of inherent existence can be arrived at by detaching from the notion of standing. To detach from the notion of standing is to not entertain the notion of standing. To detach from the notion of standing is to discontinue the formation of the notion of standing. To detach from the notion of standing is to seek the immediate absence of the notion of standing. To detach from the notion of standing is to withstand the fierceness of the arising of the notion of standing. To detach from the notion of standing is to endure patiently the absence of the notion of standing.

That which is perceived to stand is a person. The position of standing is the position of a standing person. The position of standing perceived by the mind is the notion of standing fabricated by the mind. A standing person perceived by the mind is the notion of a person fabricated by the mind. The perception of standing is caused by the presence of the notion of a person and the presence of the notion of standing. The notion of standing comes into being in the presence of the notion of a person. The arising of the notion of standing is dependent on the presence of the notion of a person. The notion of standing does not come into being in the absence of the notion of a person.

The absence of the notion of standing and the absence of the notion of inherent existence can be arrived at by detaching from the notion of a standing person. To detach from the notion of a person is to detach from both the notion of a person and the notion of standing. The notion of standing does not come into being in the absence of the notion of a person. The absence of the notion of a person is the absence of the notion of a person and the absence of the notion of standing. To detach from the notion of a person is to withstand the fierceness of the arising of the notion of a person. To detach from the notion of a person is to endure patiently the absence of the notion of a person.

To detach from the notion of standing is to arrive at the absence of the notion of standing in the presence of the notion of a person. The absence of the notion of standing and the presence of the notion of a person are the presence of the perception of a person and the absence of the perception of standing. To detach from the notion of a person is to arrive at the absence of the notion of a person and the absence of the notion of standing. The absence of the notion of a person and the absence of the notion of standing are the absence of the perception of a person and the absence of the perception of standing.

The position of standing is empty and fundamentally absent and so are the position of sitting and the position of lying down.


### Motions and positions

The motion of walking is empty and fundamentally absent. All motions are empty and fundamentally absent.

The position of standing, sitting, and lying down are empty and fundamentally absent. All positions are empty and fundamentally absent.

## Gestures and expressions

Motions and positions are empty and fundamentally absent. To understand the emptiness and fundamental absence of motions and positions is to understand the emptiness and fundamental absence of gestures and expressions. All gestures are empty and fundamentally absent. All expressions are empty and fundamentally absent.

# The emptiness of a quality and circumstance

## The emptiness of a quality

The mind perceives the presence of entities. The mind perceives the presence of a quality. A quality is an entity. The perception of a quality is the perception of an entity. The perception of a quality is the perception of inherent existence. A quality is a quality endowed with inherent existence.

A quality is devoid of inherent existence. A quality is a quality of an entity. A quality is dependent on an entity. That which is dependent on an entity cannot be endowed with inherent existence. That which cannot be endowed with inherent existence is devoid of inherent existence. A quality is devoid of inherent existence.

A quality is empty. A quality is devoid of inherent existence. The emptiness of a quality is the absence of inherent existence a quality is perceived to be endowed with. From the emptiness of a quality follows the fundamental absence of a quality. A quality is empty and fundamentally absent.

A quality perceived by the mind is the notion of a quality fabricated by the mind. Inherent existence a quality is perceived to be endowed with is the notion of inherent existence fabricated by the mind. The presence of the notion of a quality and the presence of the notion of inherent existence cause the perception of a quality endowed with inherent existence.

The emptiness and fundamental absence of a quality are revealed in the absence of the notion of a quality and the absence of the notion of inherent existence. The absence of the notion of a quality and the absence of the notion of inherent existence are the absence of a quality perceived to exist inherently and the absence of inherent existence a quality is perceived to be endowed with.

The absence of the notion of a quality and the absence of the notion of inherent existence are arrived at by detaching from the notion of a quality. To detach from the notion of a quality is to withstand the fierceness of the arising of the notion of a quality. To detach from the notion of a quality is to endure patiently the absence of the notion of a quality.


## The emptiness of a circumstance

The mind perceives the presence of entities. The mind perceives the presence of a circumstance. A circumstance is an entity. The perception of a circumstance is the perception of an entity. The perception of a circumstance is the perception of inherent existence. A circumstance is a circumstance endowed with inherent existence. A circumstance and the inherent existence indwelling in a circumstance are inseparable.

A circumstance is devoid of inherent existence. A circumstance is the coming together of circumstances. A circumstance is the coming together of entities. That which comes together constitutes a composition. The coming together of entities constitutes a composition. A circumstance is a composition. Compositions are devoid of inherent existence. A circumstance is devoid of inherent existence.

A circumstance is fundamentally absent. A circumstance is a composition of circumstances. A circumstance is a composition of entities. Circumstances do not come together and declare do constitute a circumstance. Entities do not come together and declare to constitute a circumstance. A circumstance has never come into existence. A circumstance is fundamentally absent.

All is empty. All is devoid of inherent existence. A circumstance is empty. A circumstance is devoid of inherent existence. The emptiness of a circumstance is the absence of inherent existence a circumstance is perceived to be endowed with. From the emptiness of a circumstance follows the fundamental absence of a circumstance. A circumstance is empty and fundamentally absent.

A circumstance perceived by the mind is the notion of a circumstance fabricated by the mind. Inherent existence a circumstance is perceived to be endowed with is the notion of inherent existence fabricated by the mind. The presence of the notion of a circumstance and the presence of the notion of inherent existence cause the perception of a circumstance endowed with inherent existence.

The emptiness and fundamental absence of a circumstance are revealed in the absence of the notion of a circumstance and the absence of the notion of inherent existence. The absence of the notion of a circumstance and the absence of the notion of inherent existence are the absence of a circumstance perceived to exist inherently and the absence of inherent existence a circumstance is perceived to be endowed with.

The absence of the notion of a circumstance and the absence of the notion of inherent existence are arrived at by detaching from the notion of a circumstance. To detach from the notion of a circumstance is to withstand the fierceness of the arising of the notion of a circumstance. To detach from the notion of a circumstance is to endure patiently the absence of the notion of a circumstance.

# The emptiness of the mind and notions

## The emptiness of the mind

The mind is that which thinks and feels. The mind is that which is aware and present. All thoughts and feelings arise from the mind. Suffering and the cause of suffering arise from the mind. The mind is an entity. The mind is perceived to be endowed with inherent existence. To perceive the mind to be endowed with inherent existence is to perceive the mind to exist independently from everything else. To perceive the mind to be endowed with inherent existence is to perceive the mind as a separate and distinct entity. The mind is a mind endowed with inherent existence.

The mind is devoid of inherent existence. The mind is a composition of feeling, thinking, volition, and consciousness. That which is composed of feeling, thinking, volition, and consciousness is dependent on feeling, thinking, volition, and consciousness. That which is dependent on feeling, thinking, volition, and consciousness cannot exist independently from feeling, thinking, volition, and consciousness. That which cannot exist independently from feeling, thinking, volition, and consciousness cannot exist independently from everything else. That which cannot exist independently from everything else is devoid of inherent existence. The mind is devoid of inherent existence.

The mind is fundamentally absent. The mind is a composition of feeling, thinking, volition, and consciousness. Feeling, thinking, volition, and consciousness cannot constitute a mind. Feeling, thinking, volition, and consciousness cannot constitute an entity. A mind has never come into existence. The mind is fundamentally absent. A composition of feeling, thinking, volition, and consciousness has never come into existence. A composition of feeling, thinking, volition, and consciousness is fundamentally absent. The mind is not a mind, because it is a composition. The mind is a composition and therefore not a mind.

All is empty. All is devoid of inherent existence. The mind is empty. The mind is devoid of inherent existence. The emptiness of the mind is the absence of inherent existence the mind is perceived to be endowed with. From the emptiness of the mind follows the fundamental absence of the mind. The mind is fundamentally absent. Such an entity has never come into existence. That which is fundamentally absent is not. The mind is not. The mind is not a mind. That which is fundamentally absent is inexpressible. The mind is inexpressible. The emptiness and fundamental absence of the mind are the true nature of the mind.

The perception of a mind is caused by the presence of the notion of a mind. The perception of inherent existence indwelling in the mind is caused by the presence of the notion of inherent existence. The presence of the notion of a mind and the presence of the notion of inherent existence cause the perception of an inherently existent mind. It is by way of the notion of inherent existence that the mind is perceived to exist independently from everything else. It is by way of the notion of inherent existence that the mind is perceived as a separate and distinct entity.

The emptiness and fundamental absence of the mind are revealed in the absence of the notion of a mind and the absence of the notion of inherent existence. The absence of the notion of a mind and the absence of the notion of inherent existence are the absence of a mind perceived to exist inherently and the absence of inherent existence the mind is perceived to be endowed with. The absence of inherent existence the mind is perceived to be endowed with is the emptiness of the mind. The absence of the notion of a mind and the absence of the notion of inherent existence are arrived at by detaching from the notion of a mind.

To detach from the notion of a mind is to not entertain the notion of a mind. To detach from the notion of a mind is to cease the formation of the notion of a mind. To detach from the notion of a mind is to seek the immediate absence of the notion of a mind. To detach from the notion of a mind is to withstand the fierceness of the arising of the notion of a mind. To detach from the notion of a mind is to endure patiently the absence of the notion of a mind. To detach from the notion of a mind is to reveal the emptiness and fundamental absence of the mind.

## The emptiness of thoughts

The mind perceives the presence of thoughts. Thoughts are the stitching together of words. Thoughts pertain to the sixth sense object. Thinking is the coming together of the mind, thoughts, and the consciousness of the mind. A thought is an entity. A thought is perceived to be endowed with inherent existence. To perceive a thought to be endowed with inherent existence is to perceive a thought to exist independently from everything else. To perceive a thought to be endowed with inherent existence is to perceive a thought as a separate and distinct entity. A thought is a thought endowed with inherent existence. A thought and the inherent existence indwelling in a thought are inseparable.

A thought is empty. A thought is devoid of inherent existence. A thought is the stitching together of words. A thought is a composition of words. That which is composed of words is dependent on words. That which is dependent on words cannot exist independently from words. That which cannot exist independently from words cannot exist independently from everything else. That which cannot exist independently from everything else cannot be endowed with inherent existence. That which cannot be endowed with inherent existence is devoid of inherent existence. That which is devoid of inherent existence is empty. A thought is devoid of inherent existence. A thought is empty.

A thought is fundamentally absent. A thought is a composition of words. Words cannot constitute a thought. Words cannot constitute a composition of words. A word can only constitute a word. A word can only constitute itself. A word and another word and yet other words do not come together and declare to constitute a thought. They do not come together and declare to constitute an entity. A thought has never come into existence. A thought is fundamentally absent. A composition of words has never come into existence. A composition of words is fundamentally absent. A thought is not a thought, because it is a composition. A thought is a composition and therefore not a thought.

All is empty. All is devoid of inherent existence. A thought is empty. A thought is devoid of inherent existence. The emptiness of a thought

213

is the absence of inherent existence a thought is perceived to be endowed with. From the emptiness of a thought follows the fundamental absence of a thought. A thought is fundamentally absent. A thought has never come into existence. That which is fundamentally absent is not. A thought is not. A thought is not a thought. The emptiness and fundamental absence of a thought are the true nature of a thought. That which is perceived by the mind to constitute a thought is ungraspable and inexpressible. The sixth sense object is ungraspable and inexpressible.

A thought perceived by the mind is the notion of a thought fabricated by the mind. Inherent existence a thought is perceived to be endowed with is the notion of inherent existence fabricated by the mind. The presence of the notion of a thought and the presence of the notion of inherent existence cause the perception of an inherently existent thought. It is by way of the notion of inherent existence that a thought is perceived to exist independently from everything else. It is by way of the notion of inherent existence that a thought is perceived as a separate and distinct entity. The fierceness of the arising of the notion of a thought is the mind's compulsion to fabricate the notion of a thought.

The emptiness and fundamental absence of a thought are revealed in the absence of the notion of a thought and the absence of the notion of inherent existence. The absence of the notion of a thought and the absence of the notion of inherent existence are the absence of a thought perceived to exist inherently and the absence of inherent existence a thought is perceived to be endowed with. The absence of inherent existence a thought is perceived to be endowed with is the emptiness of a thought. The absence of the notion of a thought and the absence of the notion of inherent existence are arrived at by detaching from the notion of a thought.

To detach from the notion of a thought is to not entertain the notion of a thought. To detach from the notion of a thought is to cease the formation of the notion of a thought. To detach from the notion of a thought is to seek the immediate absence of the notion of a thought. To detach from the notion of a thought is to withstand the fierceness of the arising of the notion of a thought. To detach from the notion of a thought is to endure patiently the absence of the notion of a thought. To detach from the notion of a thought in the presence of a thought is to reveal that the stitching together of words is fundamentally devoid of a thought.

## The emptiness of the notion of self

The mind perceives the presence of the notion of self. The notion of self is an entity. The notion of self is perceived to be endowed with inherent existence. To perceive the notion of self to be endowed with inherent existence is to perceive the notion of self to exist independently from everything else. To perceive the notion of self to be endowed with inherent existence is to perceive the notion of self as a separate and distinct entity. The notion of self is a notion endowed with inherent existence. The notion of self and the inherent existence indwelling in the notion of self are inseparable.

All is empty. All is devoid of inherent existence. The notion of self is empty. The notion of self is devoid of inherent existence. The emptiness of the notion of self is the absence of inherent existence the notion of self is perceived to be endowed with. From the emptiness of the notion of self follows the fundamental absence of the notion of self. The notion of self is fundamentally absent. A notion of self has never come into existence. That which is fundamentally absent is not. The notion of self is not. The notion of self is not a notion of self. That which is perceived by the mind to constitute the notion of self is ungraspable and inexpressible. The sixth sense object is ungraspable and inexpressible.

The notion of self perceived by the mind is the notion of the notion of self fabricated by the mind. Inherent existence the notion of self is perceived to be endowed with is the notion of inherent existence fabricated by the mind. The presence of the notion of the notion of self and the presence of the notion of inherent existence cause the perception of an inherently existent notion of self. It is by way of the notion of inherent existence that the notion of self is perceived to exist independently from everything else. It is by way of the notion of inherent existence that the notion of self is perceived as a separate and distinct entity.

The emptiness and fundamental absence of the notion of self are revealed in the absence of the notion of the notion of self and the absence of the notion of inherent existence. The absence of the notion of the notion of self and the absence of the notion of inherent existence are the absence of a notion of self perceived to exist inherently and the absence of inherent existence the notion of self is perceived to be endowed with. The absence of inherent existence the notion of self is perceived to be endowed with is the emptiness of the notion of self. The absence of the notion of the notion of self and the absence of the notion of inherent existence are arrived at by detaching from the notion of the notion of self.

To detach from the notion of the notion of self is to not entertain the notion of the notion of self. To detach from the notion of the notion of self is to discontinue the formation of the notion of the notion of self. To detach from the notion of the notion of self is to seek the immediate absence of the notion of the notion of self. To detach from the notion of the notion of self is to withstand the fierceness of the notion of the notion of self. To detach from the notion of the notion of self is to endure patiently the absence of the notion of the notion of self.

Detachment from the notion of self is detachment from the notion of self and detachment from the notion of the notion of self.


### The notion of self

The self is a truly and inherently existent self. The notion of self is empty and fundamentally absent. That which is empty and fundamentally absent cannot constitute that which is truly and inherently existent. The notion of self cannot constitute a self.

# Grasping at emptiness

## Emptiness

Emptiness is not an entity that can be attained. Emptiness is not a notion that can be entertained.

## The thought of the emptiness of an entity

The emptiness of an entity cannot be revealed by entertaining the thought of the emptiness of an entity. The emptiness of an entity can only be revealed by detaching from the notion of inherent existence.

## The thought of the absence of inherent existence

The absence of inherent existence cannot be revealed by entertaining the thought of the absence of inherent existence. The absence of inherent existence can only be revealed by detaching from the notion of inherent existence.

## Detachment

Detachment is detachment from the notion of inherent existence and detachment from the notion of the absence of inherent existence.

# Grasping at the absence of entities

### The thought of the absence of an entity

The fundamental absence of an entity cannot be revealed by entertaining the thought of the absence of an entity.

The fundamental absence of an entity can only be revealed by cultivating detachment from the notion of an entity.

Detachment is detachment from the notion of an entity and detachment from the notion of the absence of an entity.


### The thought of the absence of the self

The fundamental absence of the self cannot be revealed by entertaining the thought of the absence of the self.

The fundamental absence of the self can only be revealed by cultivating detachment from the notion of self.

Detachment is detachment from the notion of self and detachment from the notion of the absence of the self.


### The thought of the absence of people

The fundamental absence of people cannot be revealed by entertaining the thought of the absence of people.

The fundamental absence of people can only be revealed by cultivating detachment from the notion of people.

Detachment is detachment from the notion of people and detachment from the notion of the absence of people.


### In emptiness

The absence of the notion of inherent existence is the absence of the notion of an entity and the absence of the notion of the absence of an entity.

# Detachment in the sixth dust

## Detachment in the presence of thoughts

The mind perceives entities in the presence of thoughts. Thoughts are the stitching together of words. Thoughts pertain to the sixth sense object. Notions are the sixth sense object. Thoughts come into being by way of thinking. Thinking is the coming together of the mind, thoughts, and the consciousness of the mind.

The mind perceives entities in the presence of thoughts. The perception of entities is caused by the presence of notions of entities. Notions of entities pertain to the sixth sense object. Notions of entities come into being by way of thinking. Thinking is the coming together of the mind, notions of entities, and the consciousness of the mind.

The presence of thoughts conditions the arising of notions of entities. The coming together of the mind, thoughts, and the consciousness of the mind conditions the coming together of the mind, notions of entities, and the consciousness of the mind. Thinking gives rise to thinking. Notions of entities arise in the presence of thoughts. Entities are perceived in the presence of thoughts.

The perception of entities in the presence of thoughts can be ceased by ceasing the formation of thoughts. To cease the formation of thoughts is to arrive at the absence of thoughts and the absence of notions of entities. Notions of entities that arise in the presence of thoughts do not come into being in the absence of thoughts. The absence of thoughts is the absence of a myriad of notions of entities.

The perception of entities in the presence of thoughts can be ceased by ceasing the formation of notions of entities in the presence of thoughts. To cease the formation of notions of entities in the presence of thoughts is to withstand the fierceness of notions of entities in the presence of thoughts.

The perception of entities in the presence of thoughts can also be ceased by ceasing the formation of the notion of inherent existence in the presence of thoughts. To cease the formation of the notion of inherent existence in the presence of thoughts is to withstand the fierceness of the notion of inherent existence in the presence of thoughts.

To cease the formation of notions of entities in the presence of thoughts is to reveal that thoughts are fundamentally devoid of entities. To cease the formation of notions of entities in the presence of thoughts is to reveal that thoughts are fundamentally pure and quiescent.

# Mindfulness of sound and form

## Mindfulness of sound

Mindfulness, awareness, and endurance are the three essentials for cultivating detachment from the notion of inherent existence and all notions of entities. Mindfulness is the first essential. Mindfulness is presence of mind. To be mindful is to be mindful of the presence of a sense object. To be mindful is to be mindful of sound.

Sound is the second sense object. Sound is that which is perceived by the ears. Hearing is the coming together of the ears, sound, and the consciousness of the ears. To be mindful of sound is to be aware that the ears are perceiving. To be mindful of sound is to be aware that hearing takes place. Mindfulness of sound is the absence of wandering thoughts, for the mind can only perceive one sense object at a time. From moment to moment, the mind is aware of the presence of sound. From moment to moment, the mind is observant of the presence of sound. Whenever the mind is not aware of the presence of sound, it must quickly return to the presence of sound. Whenever the mind is distracted by wandering thoughts, it must quickly return to the presence of sound.

The mind may at first cultivate mindfulness of sound by listening to the sound of a river, the rustle of leaves, or the sound of rain. The mind may then cultivate mindfulness of sound while the ears come together with all kinds of sound. Mindfulness of sound is essential for cultivating detachment in the dust of sound. Hearing is the foremost way.

## Mindfulness of form

Mindfulness, awareness, and endurance are the three essentials for cultivating detachment from the notion of inherent existence and all notions of entities. Mindfulness is the first essential. Mindfulness is presence of mind. To be mindful is to be mindful of the presence of a sense object. To be mindful is to be mindful of form.

Form is the first sense object. Form is that which is perceived by the eyes. Seeing is the coming together of the eyes, form, and the consciousness of the eyes. To be mindful of form is to be aware that the eyes are perceiving. To be mindful of form is to be aware that seeing takes place. Mindfulness of form is the absence of wandering thoughts, for the mind can only perceive one sense object at a time. From moment to moment, the mind is aware of the presence of form. From moment to moment, the mind is observant of the presence of form. Whenever the mind is not aware of the presence of form, it must quickly return to the presence of form. Whenever the mind is distracted by wandering thoughts, it must quickly return to the presence of form.

The mind may at first cultivate mindfulness of form while the body and the eyes are facing a wall. The mind may then cultivate mindfulness of form while the eyes come together with all kinds of form. Mindfulness of form is essential for cultivating detachment in the dust of form.

# Mindfulness and endurance

## Notions of entities

Mindfulness, awareness, and endurance are the three essentials for cultivating detachment from notions of entities. Mindfulness is presence of mind. Awareness is awareness of the presence of notions of entities. Endurance is endurance of the absence of notions of entities. The presence of mindfulness is the absence of wandering thoughts. The presence of mindfulness is, however, not the absence of notions of entities. Notions of entities come into being in the presence of wandering thoughts as well as in the absence of wandering thoughts. Notions of entities arise in the absence of mindfulness as well as in the presence of mindfulness. Mindfulness is the foundation of the way. Endurance is the way. The absence of wandering thoughts is the foundation of the way. Detachment from all notions of entities is the way.

## The notion of inherent existence

Mindfulness, awareness, and endurance are the three essentials for cultivating detachment from the notion of inherent existence. Mindfulness is presence of mind. Awareness is awareness of the presence of the notion of inherent existence. Endurance is endurance of the absence of the notion of inherent existence. The presence of mindfulness is the absence of wandering thoughts. The presence of mindfulness is, however, not the absence of the notion of inherent existence. The notion of inherent existence comes into being in the presence of wandering thoughts as well as in the absence of wandering thoughts. The notion of inherent existence arises in the absence of mindfulness as well as in the presence of mindfulness. Mindfulness is the foundation of the way. Endurance is the way. The absence of wandering thoughts is the foundation of the way. Detachment from the notion of inherent existence is the way.

# The notion of inherent existence

## Awareness

The three essentials for cultivating detachment from the notion of inherent existence are mindfulness, awareness, and endurance. Awareness is the second essential. Awareness is awareness of the presence of the notion of inherent existence. The mind that seeks to be aware of the notion of inherent existence must seek within itself. The mind must reflect back. To be aware of the notion of inherent existence is to reflect back and to discern the presence of the notion of inherent existence. To be aware of the notion of inherent existence is to reflect back and to mindfully observe the presence of the notion of inherent existence.

## A feeling of presence

The notion of inherent existence arises from the mind. It comes into being way of thinking. Thinking is the coming together of the mind, the notion of inherent existence, and the consciousness of the mind. The notion of inherent existence is by itself not a conceptual notion. It is by itself not a unit of thought or language. The notion of inherent existence can be described as a feeling of mind. This feeling of mind is by itself neither pleasant nor unpleasant. It is by itself neutral and indistinct. The notion of inherent existence can be described as a feeling of presence. It is a feeling that says, "something is present."

For example, a father tells his son that he has a gift for him inside his fist. The son expects something inside his father's fist. His mind gives rise to the feeling that says, "something is present inside my father's fist." The feeling of presence is present. The notion of inherent existence is present. The father opens his fist and the son notices that there is nothing in his father's hand. The feeling that says, "something is present," vanishes at once. The feeling of presence is absent. The notion of inherent existence is absent.

For example, a merchant sells various goods to customers. He says to one of his customers, "I sell you this valuable good," and he draws with his finger a circle in empty space. The customer believes that there is something and his mind gives rise to the feeling that says, "something is present." The feeling of presence is present. The notion of inherent existence is present. The customer realizes that there is nothing and the feeling that says, "something is present," vanishes at once. The feeling of presence is absent. The notion of inherent existence is absent.

### Space in the east

The notion of inherent existence is like space in the east. To perceive space in the east is to perceive a feeling of presence. The feeling of presence is the notion of inherent existence. To perceive space in the east is to perceive the notion of inherent existence.

The notion of inherent existence is like space in the south, west, and north. To perceive space in the south, west, and north is to perceive a feeling of presence. The feeling of presence is the notion of inherent existence. To perceive space in the south, west, and north is to perceive the notion of inherent existence.

The notion of inherent existence is like space in the zenith and in the nadir. To perceive space in the zenith and in the nadir is to perceive a feeling of presence. The feeling of presence is the notion of inherent existence. To perceive space in the zenith and in the nadir is to perceive the notion of inherent existence.

### Flower in the sky

The notion of inherent existence is like a flower in the sky. A flower in the sky is a flower made of air. To perceive a flower made of air is to perceive a feeling of presence. The feeling of presence is the notion of inherent existence. To perceive a flower in the sky is to perceive the notion of inherent existence.

# Habit of mind

### The notion of an entity

The mind perceives the presence of entities. The perception of an entity is caused by the formation and presence of the notion of an entity. The mind gives rise to the notion of an entity and it mistakes the presence of the notion of an entity for a truly existent entity. The formation of notions of entities is a habit of mind. The mind has been fabricating notions of entities since time without beginning. Notions of entities arise fast. Notions of entities arise fiercely. The fierceness of the arising of the notion of an entity is the mind's compulsion to fabricate the notion of an entity.

The mind's habit of fabricating the notion of an entity can be ceased. The habit of fabricating the notion of an entity is ceased by cultivating detachment from the notion of an entity. The habit is ceased by ceasing the habit. To withstand again and again the fierceness of the arising of the notion of an entity is to gradually cease the mind's habit of fabricating the notion of an entity. To endure again and again the absence of the notion of an entity is to gradually cease the mind's habit of fabricating the notion of an entity.

### The self, people, and the body

The formation of the notion of self is a habit of mind. The mind's habit of fabricating the notion of self can be ceased by cultivating detachment from the notion of self.

The formation of the notion of people is a habit of mind. The mind's habit of fabricating the notion of people can be ceased by cultivating detachment from the notion of people.

The formation of the notion of a body is a habit of mind. The mind's habit of fabricating the notion of a body can be ceased by cultivating detachment from the notion of a body.

### The notion of inherent existence

The mind perceives the presence of inherent existence. The perception of inherent existence is caused by the formation and presence of the notion of inherent existence. The formation of the notion of inherent existence is a habit of mind. The mind has been fabricating the notion of inherent existence since time without beginning. The notion of inherent existence arises fast. The notion of inherent existence arises fiercely. The fierceness of the arising of the notion of inherent existence is the mind's compulsion to fabricate the notion of inherent existence.

The mind's habit of fabricating the notion of inherent existence can be ceased. The habit of fabricating the notion of inherent existence is ceased by cultivating detachment from the notion of inherent existence. The habit is ceased by ceasing the habit. To withstand again and again the fierceness of the arising of the notion of inherent existence is to gradually cease the mind's habit of fabricating the notion of inherent existence. To endure again and again the absence of the notion of inherent existence is to gradually cease the mind's habit of fabricating the notion of inherent existence.

# Detachment

### Notions of entities

Detachment is the way. Detachment is detachment from notions of entities. The mind may at first cultivate detachment from notions of small entities. It may then cultivate detachment from notions of large entities. The mind may at first cultivate detachment from notions of intangible entities. It may then cultivate detachment from notions of tangible entities. The mind may at first cultivate detachment from notions of inanimate entities. It may then cultivate detachment from notions of animate entities. The mind may at first cultivate detachment from notions of circumstances that are pleasant. It may then cultivate detachment from notions of circumstances that are unpleasant.

### The notion of a large entity

Detachment is the way. Detachment is detachment from notions of small entities. Detachment is detachment from notions of large entities. The formation of the notion of a large entity is difficult to cease. The difficulty in detaching from the notion of a large entity does not arise from a large entity itself, for a large entity has never come into existence. The difficulty in detaching from the notion of a large entity stems from the fierceness of the arising of the notion of a large entity. The fierceness of the arising of the notion of a large entity is the mind's compulsion to fabricate the notion of a large entity. The difficulty in detaching from the notion of a large entity arises entirely from the mind. To detach from the notion of a large entity is to withstand boldly and thoroughly the fierceness of the notion of a large entity. To detach from the notion of a large entity is to oppose with all one's strength the mind's compulsion to fabricate the notion of a large entity.

## Complete scenery

The mind that cultivates detachment must cover the complete scenery. An entity perceived by the mind is the notion of an entity fabricated by the mind. Inherent existence perceived by the mind is the notion of inherent existence fabricated by the mind. Each notion of an entity comes into being in the presence of the notion of inherent existence. The presence of multiple notions of entities is the presence of multiple notions of inherent existence. To arrive at the absence of all notions of entities, the mind must discontinue the formation of all notions of entities. To arrive at the absence of the notion of inherent existence, the mind must discontinue the formation of all notions of entities. The mind that cultivates detachment must cover the complete scenery.

## Sword of wisdom

The mind that cultivates detachment is like a sword. The sword is a sword that cuts through the presence of notions of entities. The sword is a sword that cuts through the perception of truly existent entities. The mind's strength to withstand is like the sharpness of the sword. To withstand is to withstand the fierceness of the arising of notions of entities. To withstand is to oppose the mind's compulsion to fabricate notions of entities. The mind's strength to withstand must be refined over and over. It is like honing and polishing the edge of the sword. To cultivate detachment from all thoughts and all feelings is to hone and polish the sword. To cultivate detachment from the notion of inherent existence and all notions of entities is to hone and polish the sword.

# Subjugating the mind

## Feelings

The fierceness of the arising of desire is the place to apply oneself. To withstand the fierceness of desire is to cease the affliction of desire. To withstand the fierceness of desire is to subjugate and conquer the mind.

The fierceness of the arising of hatred is the place to apply oneself. To withstand the fierceness of hatred is to cease the affliction of hatred. To withstand the fierceness of hatred is to subjugate and conquer the mind.

The fierceness of the arising of arrogance is the place to apply oneself. To withstand the fierceness of arrogance is to cease the affliction of arrogance. To withstand the fierceness of arrogance is to subjugate and conquer the mind.

## Perception

The fierceness of the arising of the notion of self is the place to apply oneself. To withstand the fierceness of the notion of self is to cease the affliction of ignorance. To withstand the fierceness of the notion of self is to subjugate and conquer the mind.

The fierceness of the arising of the notion of people is the place to apply oneself. To withstand the fierceness of the notion of people is to cease the affliction of ignorance. To withstand the fierceness of the notion of people is to subjugate and conquer the mind.

The fierceness of the arising of the notion of a body is the place to apply oneself. To withstand the fierceness of the notion of a body is to cease the affliction of ignorance. To withstand the fierceness of the notion of a body is to subjugate and conquer the mind.

# Vigor

## The notion of self and people

The perfection of vigor is the cultivation of vigor. To cultivate the perfection of vigor is to resolve to break through the impenetrableness of the notion of self and people. To cultivate the perfection of vigor is to withstand boldly and thoroughly the fierceness of the arising of the notion of self and people. To cultivate the perfection of vigor is to oppose with all one's strength the mind's compulsion to fabricate the notion of self and people. To cultivate the perfection of vigor is to constantly abide in the absence of the notion of self and people. To cultivate the perfection of vigor is to never retreat from the absence of the notion of self and people. To cultivate the perfection of vigor is to endure patiently the absence of the notion of self and people.

## The notion of inherent existence

The perfection of vigor is the cultivation of vigor. To cultivate the perfection of vigor is to resolve to break through the impenetrableness of the notion of inherent existence. To cultivate the perfection of vigor is to withstand boldly and thoroughly the fierceness of the arising of the notion of inherent existence. To cultivate the perfection of vigor is to oppose with all one's strength the mind's compulsion to fabricate the notion of inherent existence. To cultivate the perfection of vigor is to constantly abide in the absence of the notion of inherent existence. To cultivate the perfection of vigor is to never retreat from the absence of the notion of inherent existence. To cultivate the perfection of vigor is to endure patiently the absence of the notion of inherent existence.

# Sovereignty

## The perfection of meditation

The perfection of meditation is detachment and sovereignty. The perfection of meditation is the fifth perfection. Detachment is detachment from notions of entities. Sovereignty is sovereignty over notions of entities. To detach from notions of entities is to attain sovereignty over notions of entities. To endure the absence of notions of entities is to attain sovereignty over notions of entities.

## Sovereignty

Sovereignty is the state of mind in which the mind remains unmoved. The mind moves in the presence of the six dusts. The six dusts are form, sound, smell, taste, touch, and notions. To move is to grasp and dwell. To move is to cling and reject. That which causes the mind to move is the presence of notions of entities. To be moved is to be moved by the presence of notions of entities that arise in the presence of the six dusts.

To remain unmoved is to remain unmoved in the presence of the six dusts. To remain unmoved is to not entertain notions of entities in the presence of the six dusts. To not entertain notions of entities in the presence of the six dusts is to abide in sovereignty. To remain unmoved in the presence of the six dusts is to abide in sovereignty. Sovereignty is the state of mind in which the mind remains unmoved.

## Sovereignty

Sovereignty is the state of mind in which the fierceness of the arising of notions of entities is constantly withstood. Sovereignty is the state of mind in which the absence of notions of entities is patiently endured.

## Sovereignty

To abide in sovereignty, the mind must attain the ability to withstand. To withstand is to withstand the fierceness of notions of entities that arise in the presence of the six dusts. The ability to withstand can be learned and practiced. The ability to withstand can be learned and practiced by cultivating detachment from heaven and earth.

## The perfection of meditation

The perfection of meditation is detachment and sovereignty. Detachment is detachment from the notion of inherent existence. Sovereignty is sovereignty over the notion of inherent existence. To detach from the notion of inherent existence is to attain sovereignty over the notion of inherent existence.

Sovereignty is the state of mind in which the mind remains unmoved. To remain unmoved is to remain unmoved in the presence of form, sound, smell, taste, touch, and notions. To remain unmoved is to not entertain the notion of inherent existence in the presence of form, sound, smell, taste, touch, and notions.

Sovereignty is the state of mind in which the fierceness of the arising of the notion of inherent existence is constantly withstood. Sovereignty is the state of mind in which the absence of the notion of inherent existence is patiently endured.

# The true nature of all

### All is devoid of a self

The mind perceives the presence of a self. The self is fundamentally absent. All is devoid of a self. The mind perceives that which is fundamentally absent, because it fabricates a notion of that which is fundamentally absent. The presence of the notion of self shrouds the fundamental absence of the self. The fundamental absence of the self, however, remains devoid of a self. A thousand, ten thousand, and a hundred thousand notions of self cannot cause the absence of a self to be endowed with a self. The fundamental absence of the self is the true nature of the self. All is devoid of a self. The self is fundamentally absent.

### All is devoid of inherent existence

The mind perceives inherent existence. Inherent existence is fundamentally absent. All is devoid of inherent existence. The mind perceives the absence of inherent existence to be endowed with inherent existence, because it fabricates the notion of inherent existence. The presence of the notion of inherent existence shrouds the absence of inherent existence. The absence of inherent existence, however, remains devoid of inherent existence. A thousand, ten thousand, and a hundred thousand notions of inherent existence cannot cause the absence of inherent existence to be endowed with inherent existence. The absence of inherent existence is the true nature of all. All is devoid of inherent existence. Inherent existence is fundamentally absent.

234

# Investigating the origin of words

## Who is mindful of the Buddha?

To sit is to sit upright. To meditate is to be mindful. To be mindful of the Buddha is to think of the name of the Buddha. To be mindful of the Buddha is to uninterruptedly bring to mind the name of the Buddha. The mind that is well acquainted with meditating on the name of the Buddha can investigate the question "Who is mindful of the Buddha?" The question "Who is mindful of the Buddha?" is an object of meditation.

The mind must raise the question "Who is mindful of the Buddha?" as if it is sincerely seeking an answer to that question. Investigating the question in such a way gives rise to a feeling of doubt. Each time the mind raises the question, it must give rise to that feeling of doubt. The feeling of doubt is important.

Whenever the question "Who is mindful of the Buddha?" is raised, the mind must not fabricate intellectual answers. The mind must raise and investigate the question as if it is sincerely seeking an answer to that question, but it must not entertain intellectual answers. The absence of intellectual answers is important.

Whenever the mind does not investigate the question "Who is mindful of the Buddha?" it must quickly return to the question. Whenever the mind is distracted by wandering thoughts, it must quickly return to the question. The absence of wandering thoughts is the presence of mindfulness. The presence of mindfulness is the presence of the way.

From moment to moment, the mind raises the question "Who is mindful of the Buddha?" From moment to moment, the mind gives rise to a feeling of doubt. From moment to moment, the mind must not fabricate intellectual answers. To meditate is to meditate without haste. This method of meditation is known as 'investigating the origin of words'.

# Detachment in the presence of sound

### Notions of entities

Notions of entities arise in the presence of sound. Sound is that which is perceived by the ears. The ears come together with sound and the mind gives rise to notions of entities. The coming together of the ears, sound, and the consciousness of the ears conditions the coming together of the mind, notions of entities, and the consciousness of the mind. Hearing conditions thinking. Notions of entities arise in the presence of sound.

Detachment is detachment in the presence of sound. To detach from notions of entities in the presence of sound is to cultivate mindfulness, awareness, and endurance. Mindfulness is presence of mind. Mindfulness is mindfulness of sound. Awareness is awareness of the presence of notions of entities arising in the presence of sound. Endurance is endurance of the absence of notions of entities arising in the presence of sound.

### The notion of self

The notion of self arises in the presence of sound. Sound is that which is perceived by the ears. The ears come together with sound and the mind gives rise to the notion of self. The coming together of the ears, sound, and the consciousness of the ears conditions the coming together of the mind, the notion of self, and the consciousness of the mind. Hearing conditions thinking. The notion of the hearing entity arises in the presence of sound.

Detachment is detachment in the presence of sound. To cultivate detachment from the notion of self in the presence of sound is to cultivate mindfulness, awareness, and endurance. Mindfulness is presence of mind. Mindfulness is mindfulness of sound. Awareness is awareness of the presence of the notion of self arising in the presence of sound. Endurance is endurance of the absence of the notion of self arising in the presence of sound.

## The notion of people

The notion of people arises in the presence of sound. Sound is that which is perceived by the ears. The ears come together with sound and the mind gives rise to the notion of people. The coming together of the ears, sound, and the consciousness of the ears conditions the coming together of the mind, the notion of people, and the consciousness of the mind. Hearing conditions thinking. The notion of people arises in the presence of sound.

Detachment is detachment in the presence of sound. To detach from the notion of people in the presence of sound is to cultivate mindfulness, awareness, and endurance. Mindfulness is presence of mind. Mindfulness is mindfulness of sound. Awareness is awareness of the presence of the notion of people arising in the presence of sound. Endurance is endurance of the absence of the notion of people arising in the presence of sound.


## The notion of inherent existence

The notion of inherent existence arises in the presence of sound. Sound is that which is perceived by the ears. The ears come together with sound and the mind gives rise to the notion of inherent existence. The coming together of the ears, sound, and the consciousness of the ears conditions the coming together of the mind, the notion of inherent existence, and the consciousness of the mind. Hearing conditions thinking. The notion of inherent existence arises in the presence of sound.

Detachment is detachment in the presence of sound. To detach from the notion of inherent existence in the presence of sound is to cultivate mindfulness, awareness, and endurance. Mindfulness is presence of mind. Mindfulness is mindfulness of sound. Awareness is awareness of the presence of the notion of inherent existence arising in the presence of sound. Endurance is endurance of the absence of the notion of inherent existence arising in the presence of sound.

# Detachment in the presence of form

### Notions of entities

Notions of entities arise in the presence of form. Form is that which is perceived by the eyes. The eyes come together with form and the mind gives rise to notions of entities. The coming together of the eyes, form, and the consciousness of the eyes conditions the coming together of the mind, notions of entities, and the consciousness of the mind. Seeing conditions thinking. Notions of entities arise in the presence of form.

Detachment is detachment in the presence of form. To detach from notions of entities in the presence of form is to cultivate mindfulness, awareness, and endurance. Mindfulness is presence of mind. Mindfulness is mindfulness of form. Awareness is awareness of the presence of notions of entities arising in the presence of form. Endurance is endurance of the absence of notions of entities arising in the presence of form.

### The notion of self

The notion of self arises in the presence of form. Form is that which is perceived by the eyes. The eyes come together with form and the mind gives rise to the notion of self. The coming together of the eyes, form, and the consciousness of the eyes conditions the coming together of the mind, the notion of self, and the consciousness of the mind. Seeing conditions thinking. The notion of the seeing entity arises in the presence of form.

Detachment is detachment in the presence of form. To cultivate detachment from the notion of self in the presence of form is to cultivate mindfulness, awareness, and endurance. Mindfulness is presence of mind. Mindfulness is mindfulness of form. Awareness is awareness of the presence of the notion of self arising in the presence of form. Endurance is endurance of the absence of the notion of self arising in the presence of form.

### The notion of people

The notion of people arises in the presence of form. Form is that which is perceived by the eyes. The eyes come together with form and the mind gives rise to the notion of people. The coming together of the eyes, form, and the consciousness of the eyes conditions the coming together of the mind, the notion of people, and the consciousness of the mind. Seeing conditions thinking. The notion of people arises in the presence of form.

Detachment is detachment in the presence of form. To detach from the notion of people in the presence of form is to cultivate mindfulness, awareness, and endurance. Mindfulness is presence of mind. Mindfulness is mindfulness of form. Awareness is awareness of the presence of the notion of people arising in the presence of form. Endurance is endurance of the absence of the notion of people arising in the presence of form.

### The notion of a body

The notion of a body arises in the presence of form. Form is that which is perceived by the eyes. The eyes come together with form and the mind gives rise to the notion of a body. The coming together of the eyes, form, and the consciousness of the eyes conditions the coming together of the mind, the notion of a body, and the consciousness of the mind. Seeing conditions thinking. The notion of a body arises in the presence of form.

Detachment is detachment in the presence of form. To cultivate detachment from the notion of a body in the presence of form is to cultivate mindfulness, awareness, and endurance. Mindfulness is presence of mind. Mindfulness is mindfulness of form. Awareness is awareness of the presence of the notion of a body arising in the presence of form. Endurance is endurance of the absence of the notion of a body arising in the presence of form.

### The notion of inherent existence

The notion of inherent existence arises in the presence of form. Form is that which is perceived by the eyes. The eyes come together with form and the mind gives rise to the notion of inherent existence. The coming together of the eyes, form, and the consciousness of the eyes conditions the coming together of the mind, the notion of inherent existence, and the consciousness of the mind. Seeing conditions thinking. The notion of inherent existence arises in the presence of form.

Detachment is detachment in the presence of form. To detach from the notion of inherent existence in the presence of form is to cultivate mindfulness, awareness, and endurance. Mindfulness is presence of mind. Mindfulness is mindfulness of form. Awareness is awareness of the presence of the notion of inherent existence arising in the presence of form. Endurance is endurance of the absence of the notion of inherent existence arising in the presence of form.

# Detachment in the presence of touch

### The notion of a body

The notion of a body arises in the presence of touch. Touch is that which is perceived by the body. The body comes together with touch and the mind gives rise to the notion of a body. The coming together of the body, touch, and the consciousness of the body conditions the coming together of the mind, the notion of a body, and the consciousness of the mind. Feeling conditions thinking. The notion of one's own body arises in the presence of touch.

Detachment is detachment in the presence of touch. To detach from the notion of a body in the presence of touch is to cultivate mindfulness, awareness, and endurance. Mindfulness is presence of mind. Mindfulness is mindfulness of touch. Awareness is awareness of the presence of the notion of a body arising in the presence of touch. Endurance is endurance of the absence of the notion of a body arising in the presence of touch.

### The notion of inherent existence

The notion of inherent existence arises in the presence of touch. Touch is that which is perceived by the body. The body comes together with touch and the mind gives rise to the notion of inherent existence. The coming together of the body, touch, and the consciousness of the body conditions the coming together of the mind, the notion of inherent existence, and the consciousness of the mind. Feeling conditions thinking. The notion of inherent existence arises in the presence of touch.

Detachment is detachment in the presence of touch. To detach from the notion of inherent existence in the presence of touch is to cultivate mindfulness, awareness, and endurance. Mindfulness is presence of mind. Mindfulness is mindfulness of touch. Awareness is awareness of the presence of the notion of inherent existence arising in the presence of touch. Endurance is endurance of the absence of the notion of inherent existence arising in the presence of touch.

# Detachment in the presence of thoughts

### Notions of entities

Notions of entities arise in the presence of thoughts. Thoughts are the stitching together of words. Thoughts pertain to the sixth sense object. The presence of thoughts conditions the arising of notions of entities. The coming together of the mind, thoughts, and the consciousness of the mind conditions the coming together of the mind, notions of entities, and the consciousness of the mind. Thinking gives rise to thinking. Notions of entities arise in the presence of thoughts.

Detachment is detachment in the presence of thoughts. To detach from notions of entities in the presence of thoughts is to cultivate mindfulness, awareness, and endurance. Mindfulness is presence of mind. Mindfulness is mindfulness of thoughts. Awareness is awareness of the presence of notions of entities arising in the presence of thoughts. Endurance is endurance of the absence of notions of entities arising in the presence of thoughts.

### The notion of self

The notion of self arises in the presence of thoughts. Thoughts are the stitching together of words. Thoughts pertain to the sixth sense object. The presence of thoughts conditions the arising of the notion of self. The coming together of the mind, thoughts, and the consciousness of the mind conditions the coming together of the mind, the notion of self, and the consciousness of the mind. Thinking gives rise to thinking. The notion of the thinking entity arises in the presence of thoughts.

Detachment is detachment in the presence of thoughts. To cultivate detachment from the notion of self in the presence of thoughts is to cultivate mindfulness, awareness, and endurance. Mindfulness is presence of mind. Mindfulness is mindfulness of thoughts. Awareness is awareness of the presence of the notion of self arising in the presence of thoughts. Endurance is endurance of the absence of the notion of self arising in the presence of thoughts.

### The notion of inherent existence

The notion of inherent existence arises in the presence of thoughts. Thoughts are the stitching together of words. Thoughts pertain to the sixth sense object. The presence of thoughts conditions the arising of the notion of inherent existence. The coming together of the mind, thoughts, and the consciousness of the mind conditions the coming together of the mind, the notion of inherent existence, and the consciousness of the mind. Thinking gives rise to thinking. The notion of inherent existence arises in the presence of thoughts.

Detachment is detachment in the presence of thoughts. To detach from the notion of inherent existence in the presence of thoughts is to cultivate mindfulness, awareness, and endurance. Mindfulness is presence of mind. Mindfulness is mindfulness of thoughts. Awareness is awareness of the presence of the notion of inherent existence arising in the presence of thoughts. Endurance is endurance of the absence of the notion of inherent existence arising in the presence of thoughts.

# Bodhisattva

### The resolve to attain enlightenment

The Diamond Sutra says, "Subhuti, a bodhisattva should detach from and give up all notions and resolve to attain unsurpassed complete enlightenment in the absence of all notions." The word 'notion' refers to that which causes the perception of entities. That which causes the perception of entities are notions of entities. The word 'notion' also refers to that which causes the perception of inherent existence. That which causes the perception of inherent existence is the notion of inherent existence. To detach from and give up all notions is to detach from the notion of inherent existence and all notions of entities. To resolve to attain enlightenment is to resolve to attain enlightenment in the absence of the notion of inherent existence and the absence of all notions of entities.

### The bodhisattva way

To cultivate the bodhisattva way is to resolve to attain unsurpassed complete enlightenment in the absence of the notion of inherent existence and the absence of all notions of entities. To cultivate the bodhisattva way is to vow to liberate all sentient beings in the absence of the notion of inherent existence and the absence of all notions of entities. To cultivate the bodhisattva way is to benefit and enlighten self and others in the absence of the notion of inherent existence and the absence of all notions of entities. To cultivate the bodhisattva way is to cultivate compassion in the absence of the notion of inherent existence and the absence of all notions of entities. To cultivate the bodhisattva way is to cultivate the six perfections in the absence of the notion of inherent existence and the absence of all notions of entities. To cultivate the bodhisattva way is to cultivate all virtues in the absence of the notion of inherent existence and the absence of all notions of entities. To cultivate the bodhisattva way is to liberate all sentient beings in the absence of the notion of inherent existence and the absence of all notions of entities.

# The self, a person, and the body

### The emptiness of the self

The mind perceives the presence of a self. The self is an entity. The self is perceived to be endowed with inherent existence. To perceive the self to be endowed with inherent existence is to perceive the self to exist independently from everything else. The self is a self endowed with inherent existence.

All is empty. All is devoid of inherent existence. The self is empty. The self is devoid of inherent existence. The emptiness of the self is the absence of inherent existence the self is perceived to be endowed with. From the emptiness of the self follows the fundamental absence of the self. The self is empty and fundamentally absent.

The self perceived by the mind is the notion of self fabricated by the mind. Inherent existence the self is perceived to be endowed with is the notion of inherent existence fabricated by the mind. The presence of the notion of self and the presence of the notion of inherent existence cause the perception of an inherently existent self.

The emptiness and fundamental absence of the self are revealed in the absence of the notion of self and the absence of the notion of inherent existence. The absence of the notion of self and the absence of the notion of inherent existence are the absence of a self perceived to exist inherently and the absence of inherent existence the self is perceived to be endowed with.

The absence of the notion of self and the absence of the notion of inherent existence are arrived at by detaching from the notion of self. To detach from the notion of self is to not entertain the notion of self. To detach from the notion of self is to endure patiently the absence of the notion of self.

## The emptiness of a person

The mind perceives the presence of a person. A person is an entity. A person is perceived to be endowed with inherent existence. To perceive a person to be endowed with inherent existence is to perceive a person to exist by itself and in itself. A person is a person endowed with inherent existence.

All is empty. All is devoid of inherent existence. A person is empty. A person is devoid of inherent existence. The emptiness of a person is the absence of inherent existence a person is perceived to be endowed with. From the emptiness of a person follows the fundamental absence of a person. A person is empty and fundamentally absent.

A person perceived by the mind is the notion of a person fabricated by the mind. Inherent existence a person is perceived to be endowed with is the notion of inherent existence fabricated by the mind. The presence of the notion of a person and the presence of the notion of inherent existence cause the perception of an inherently existent person.

The emptiness and fundamental absence of a person are revealed in the absence of the notion of a person and the absence of the notion of inherent existence. The absence of the notion of a person and the absence of the notion of inherent existence are the absence of a person perceived to exist inherently and the absence of inherent existence a person is perceived to be endowed with.

The absence of the notion of a person and the absence of the notion of inherent existence are arrived at by detaching from the notion of a person. To detach from the notion of a person is to not entertain the notion of a person. To detach from the notion of a person is to endure patiently the absence of the notion of a person.

## The emptiness of the body

The mind perceives the presence of a body. The body is an entity. The body is perceived to be endowed with inherent existence. To perceive the body to be endowed with inherent existence is to perceive the body as a separate and distinct entity. The body is a body endowed with inherent existence.

All is empty. All is devoid of inherent existence. The body is empty. The body is devoid of inherent existence. The emptiness of the body is the absence of inherent existence the body is perceived to be endowed with. From the emptiness of the body follows the fundamental absence of the body. The body is empty and fundamentally absent.

The body perceived by the mind is the notion of a body fabricated by the mind. Inherent existence the body is perceived to be endowed with is the notion of inherent existence fabricated by the mind. The presence of the notion of a body and the presence of the notion of inherent existence cause the perception of an inherently existent body.

The emptiness and fundamental absence of the body are revealed in the absence of the notion of a body and the absence of the notion of inherent existence. The absence of the notion of a body and the absence of the notion of inherent existence are the absence of a body perceived to exist inherently and the absence of inherent existence the body is perceived to be endowed with.

The absence of the notion of a body and the absence of the notion of inherent existence are arrived at by detaching from the notion of a body. To detach from the notion of a body is to not entertain the notion of a body. To detach from the notion of a body is to endure patiently the absence of the notion of a body.

# The meaning of the way

### The cessation of the mind

All is empty and all is mind. The cessation of the mind reveals the emptiness of all.

### The notion of self

The notion of self is the fundamental cause of all suffering. To cultivate detachment from the notion of self is to cease the fundamental cause of all suffering.

### The meaning of the way

To awaken to the absence of the notion of inherent existence is to reveal the meaning of the way. To endure patiently the absence of the notion of inherent existence is to uphold the meaning of the way.